Why are we afraid to be who we really are?

Why do we seek to measure up to other's
expectations instead of our own?

Why do we so freely hand our power
over to someone else?

In the process of coming to terms with one's truth
and finally feeling comfortable in one's own skin,
there awaits an even greater reward.

The gift of YOU.

Coloring Outside the Lines reveals how to get to this place—how to come to terms with one's true self, and how to know total empowerment.

Coloring Outside the Lines takes an honest and heartfelt look at one man's story of growing up in the deep, conservative south. Mark Hyde's childhood was unique in the fact that he was one of a set of triplets from a broken home. He constantly tried to do things by other people's standards and not his own. He lost himself in religious dogma, six years of Baptist education, a feeble effort at marriage, and two suicide attempts. It was a desperate struggle to fit in.

It is a story of the extremes to which we often go

to not disappoint other people. He knows all too well what it's like to be uncomfortable in one's own skin, to seek after other people's ideas of truth instead of his own.

This is Mark's account of walking away from his entire support system that defined his self-worth as a person.

He had to do it for his own sake; he had to be true to himself. It was the only way to find comfort in his own skin and as a result, embrace his personal truth.

You can be true to yourself.

You have a right and a freedom.

Take heart that it can be done and done beautifully. This is a story of how to get to that place we all desire, complete assurance of who and what we are.

COLORING

OUTSIDE

THE LINES

One gay man's journey to self-acceptance and spiritual awakening

MARK
HYDE

REGAL
PRESS

Coloring Outside the Lines
Copyright © November, 2006 by Mark Hyde

Most scripture references within are from The New International Version (NIV), ©1973, 1978, 1984 by the International Bible Society, Zondervan.

10-Digit ISBN: 0-9789301-0-X
13-Digit ISBN: 978-0-9789301-0-3
Library of Congress Control Number: 2006936680

Cover and art work: Manjari Graphics
Layout: J. L. Saloff
Fonts: Calisto, Worstveld Sting, URW Alcuin, Bank Gothic

First Edition

Printed in the United States of America on acid free paper.

CONTENTS

DEDICATION:

I dedicate this book to my older brother Norman and my triplet brothers, Matthew and Michael. Our life has not been an easy one. Thank you for making the journey with me and for giving me such a unique arena in which to begin this search for myself. I love you. To Christina, the sister I never knew, I look forward to finally meeting you one day.

To my friend, soul mate, and confidant Robert Manning and his truly amazing family. You have treated me as one of your own. You're good people and I love you all. Robert, I would not trade the amazing bond we share for all the riches of this world for they would pale in comparison.

Leslie Joy, you are a gift to me. Thank you for being a mirror and for emulating the beautiful qualities that do exist in this world.

This book is also dedicated to you the reader. I am honored to share with you. May you continue to persevere on your own path of self-discovery. You cannot fail if you don't give up.

Remember always that
You not only have the
Right to be an individual,
You have an obligation
To be one.

Eleanor Roosevelt

Introduction

As I sit here and write I feel almost selfish. This is an account of taking back my life and reclaiming what is rightfully mine. I had sought my entire life to please others. As noble as a path that might have been, there was immense emptiness and dissatisfaction with the whole process. Deep within, I knew that I was going against my own intuitive will. How could I stand up for what I felt was right and proper for me? It was a constant struggle inside my heart, mind, and spirit. How many different people could possibly live inside of me? I wanted the inner turmoil to go away. I was tired of being noble and correct. I was exhausted from trying to live up to other people's expectations for my own life.

If I was not what these good intentioned people wanted me to be, then who was I? That question scared the hell out of me. It also challenged, and recharged me about this whole idea of life. On the one hand, it was terribly frightening, but on the other, it was very exciting. My life could be anything I wanted it to be. Could I do it? Would I do it? All the drive I remembered I had as a child came rushing back. I had run this treadmill of approval-seeking for years. I had been coerced onto it at a very early age and now I wanted off. For many years, it had to do with wanting to please others and being accepted, and little to do with accepting myself.

Where do I go from here and in what direction? Like a dog suddenly freed from its chain, I had a choice: run back to my owners or blaze new trails. It was frightening to say the least. I struggled my entire life to have my own identity and path. It now lay before me, and the decision to follow was completely mine. I chose to step forward: one painstaking and awkward step at a time. I felt like a child learning to walk. I felt fear and exhilaration. I was entering the unknown, but also the unblemished. I could proceed in fear, or I could journey in the total excitement of finally being in the driver's seat. It felt right. It felt authentic. It felt completely mine.

It has been a journey, a difficult, bleak, and lonely one at times. I know what it's like to strive for perfection and fail miserably for all to see. I have experienced first-hand what it's like to be in the darkest depths of despair and believe that life could no longer be endured. But I also realize what it is like to have made it through, and am better for it. I can honestly say that I would not change a thing. I accept, embrace, and own it all for I am right where I want to be. I have learned of a greater acceptance, compassion, and sense of validation. I intimately know complete surrender and the full extent of God's true grace in my life.

Throughout this entire creative process there has been ample self-doubt about my abilities to write this book. What do I have to offer? Will anyone even care to read it? What if I'm out of my league? I chose not to heed these fears and remained true to my called task. By writing my story I feel that I have already succeeded. In this book, I give you truth, honesty, and sincerity; I give you my heart. I am proud of what I offer you in the following pages of *Coloring Outside The Lines.*

CHAPTER 1

CHILDHOOD

This whole journey began when I was born into a family as one of a set of triplets. We were born Mark Dennis, Matthew Dale and Michael David Hyde; the third pregnancy for my German born mother and ex-military father. We arrived four days before my oldest brother's fourth birthday, and I am quite sure he was not too happy. About a year prior, my parents had lost their only daughter at the age of two. She died, we believe, from an unknown concussion, while in her sleep. She had fallen on the back steps of their home. This loss would take a toll on our lives for years to come.

My entire childhood was clouded by this terrible loss. My parents never talked about it. My only recollections were photos of my sister and my older brother as children. And then there were the photos of my sister lying in her casket, looking peaceful and serene. As if she was only asleep.

I have fond memories of attending the Head Start Program for underprivileged kids. My favorite part of that experience was being given Brown Cow ice cream bars after our daily naps. I cherish the memories of the times when my dad would pick me up and draw me to his chest. I can still remember the smell of Old Spice and the sensation of his five o'clock shadow against my face. These are the tender memories of my dad as a father. My parents separated and divorced somewhere around 1973. I never really knew the reasons why, but I did know that my idea of family was shattered. And it was at the time that I needed it most. In all honesty, I only have one vague recollection of my parents being happy. Needless to say, it is a memory I hold dear. I do remember seeing photos of the big snowstorm that came through Manning, South Carolina, in 1973. We were outside playing in the snow, and my parents seem to be having an enjoyable time. Shortly thereafter, everything, very much like the blizzard, becomes tempest.

As best as I can remember, my dad was absent. We spent a short time at an aunt's house (my dad's sister) down the street. Soon afterward, we moved to a farmhouse out in the country several miles away. It was surrounded by cornfields and other crops. I can still recall the sweet smell of tomatoes and cucumbers that lingered. There were pigs and a grain silo. Oddly enough, this would be the same area where my mother would be killed in a car crash some thirty years later. The farm was an awkward place. I, along with my brothers, really had no idea of what was going on. I guess my favorite memories of that period were of waking up on Saturday mornings, and having doughnuts and chocolate milk, the generic glazed doughnuts, packaged in a clear plastic container, for

$1.99. These are the good moments that emerge to the surface.

I do know that about the same time my mom had a new male friend that started coming around the farm to visit. His name was Bruce. I only remember meeting him once or twice. The first time he came by, he brought fireworks with him for us to enjoy. He seemed nice enough. Sometime thereafter, we found out that they were getting married when we were being taken to our dad's home in North Carolina for a few days. I can't remember exactly who told us. Once we got back to South Carolina, we were all living together in a three-bedroom, one bath apartment in Sumter, on Bowman Street. My next recollection is of my new step dad enrolling my brothers and me at Crosswell Elementary School just a few blocks away from our new home. I remember the principal's name was Eddie Myers. He was a strikingly handsome man, in his thirties. He seemed to be genuine and caring. This was a new concept to this six-year-old little boy. Crosswell Elementary was a formidable place. We finally had a refuge. It was a place of stability, structure, and learning.

My older brother Norman, was ten years old, so when we started first grade he was in the fifth. I cannot say that we had a great relationship back then. In my little mind, he always seemed to be just outside the picture. He would eventually, at the age of sixteen, move out on his own. I've always been curious about what life was like for him, how he felt about his three younger brothers, and what he perceived about all the events that had transpired in previous years.

Elementary school was a hodgepodge of experiences. I remember my first-grade teacher, a big, jovial black woman named Miss Jackson. I remember making my first A in spelling in third grade. I remember my PE coach, Mr. Silva, and my fifth-grade teacher, Mrs. McDonald. Life in elementary school as a triplet was odd. Never could I just be Mark. I was always referred to as one of the Hyde triplets. Everywhere I turned, there was Matthew or Michael or some reference to them. Lab was also a memorable part of my elementary school experience. I'm not really sure if we had learning disabilities or just behavioral problems. There was a whole lot going on.

Much of it I did not understand. It was as if it was someone else's life, and I just happened to be viewing it from the sidelines. In fifth grade, Mrs. McDonald taught us phrases like, "Let sleeping dogs lie," "It's no use in crying over spilt milk," and "You can't teach an old dog new tricks."

In this new address we called home, there was an older woman in her sixties that moved in next door. Her name was Rosa Scott. She would change our lives forever. Mrs. Scott was a sweet, southern woman who had grown kids of her own and several grandchildren that were our age and younger. She took a liking to us as we did to her. She became a surrogate grandmother. Early one Sunday morning, we saw her dressed up and heading somewhere. We asked her where she was off to and she told us to church. We wanted to go with her. She asked our mother if we could join her. My mother said it was too late to go that day, but that we could go the following Sunday. The next Sunday rolled around and she loaded us up in her blue Ford Fairlane and off we went to Salem Avenue Baptist Church. This experience opened up for my brothers and me a whole new world. In this newfound community, we were loved, accepted, and nurtured. There were minor behavioral problems along the way, but the nurturing and parenting that we received from that church proved immeasurable. I truly believe I am the man I am today because of that church, and people like Rosa Scott, who went out of their way to show love to three needy boys.

Without a doubt, the church was a stabilizing force in my earliest and most formative years. I don't know how I would have turned out or where I would be, if not for this positive influence in my life. We did enjoy going to church on a regular basis, but as the years passed, we became more reluctant. During these times, we were forced to go by our mother. She herself was not religious. She had been raised Roman Catholic as a child in Germany. She had fled her parents' authority, met my father, got pregnant, and married. They had their first child in Germany, just a few months later in June of 1964. Immediately there-after, they left for the States. She was twenty three and he, twenty-one.

In the church, I found my source of identity. It was a place where I could belong. We would go on field trips and outings, things we could not have done otherwise. Church became my whole life. We were there every time the doors opened. Sunday mornings,

Sunday nights, youth choir practice, Wednesday night services, and Tuesday night visitation. It had become a way of life. A week of Vacation Bible School was how our summers always began.

And then there was a week of youth camp during midsummer that was always awesome. We did fun activities like swimming, hiking, canoeing, and arts and crafts. All the fun things that a child loves to do. The services, each night, were intense and emotional. It was during one of these evening camp services at Camp Bonnie Doone, in Walterboro, South Carolina, that I asked Jesus to come into my heart. I had asked for forgiveness of my sins and professed my faith in Him. My triplet brothers did the same that night. When we got back to Sumter, our church was ecstatic that the triplets had been saved. We were baptized shortly thereafter, and joined the church as full-fledged members.

During this whole process, my mom's second marriage to Bruce was a tumultuous one. He was a successful barber in town, and at one point, even owned his own shop. Things were finally looking promising. We had moved into a larger house on Loring Place, just a block away from our old apartment. I believe we were in fourth or fifth grade. As time went on, my stepfather became physically abusive to my mother. He would drink heavily, they would get into arguments and then it would get physical.

As time went on, these occurrences happened on a more frequent basis. I often wondered why my mother would stay in this abusive relationship. Why would she not just leave him? These are the thoughts that run rampant through a child's mind. I wanted to make things better for her. As an adult, I can look back and realize her dire situation. Where was she to go? How was she to survive? You see, my mom had worked in a factory her entire life. She spoke very limited English, and had four children of her own to feed and care for. It puts things in perspective, doesn't it?

It was Bruce who was the first to point out my obvious "unboylike behavior." He was relentless and quite often cruel. I was a sensitive little boy and had begun to show my first signs of being gay. He had no problem pointing this out and calling me derogatory names. This was painful, especially coming from the man that I called Dad.

In the summer of 1981, just after finishing our seventh grade in middle school, our family split apart. My mother had been involved in an extramarital affair. It was also during this time that a family friend had come to live with us who was dying of cancer. We were spending our summer holidays looking after and caring for him. I was the one to initially suspect that something was going on. My mom would get phone calls. A strange man would drop her off after work. I knew what she was doing was wrong, and I informed my stepfather. The shit really hit the fan. The very day that all of this came out, my mom scowled at me with a drawn fist and gave me the meanest look I had ever seen. I truly was afraid for my life. My stepfather again became physical with my mother. She left our home for her own safety.

My mom called the man whom she was involved with. He picked her up a few blocks up the street. I don't know where they went. I did find out a few days later, that he too, was married and had a family of his own. And to make things even worse, we learned that one of his daughters was a classmate of ours. "Awkward" does not even begin to describe the situation when we would see each other at school. We never talked about it.

I vividly remember that a few days later, after all of this had been revealed, I went to go visit my mother at a local hotel in town. I was terribly nervous. Was she going to be angry, hate me, and hit me? Those thoughts flooded my mind. But I also knew that I wanted to see her. I had to know that she was all right. I wanted her to know that I loved her still and did not hate her for what she had done. Even at twelve years old, I could see that a lot of circumstances had led up to the affair. It had not been entirely her fault. When I walked into that hotel room, I saw a distraught and broken woman whose spirit had been shattered. It ripped my heart out. Even as a preteen, I began to see how life can take its toll. It was as if her pain and heartache were my own. I had always had this innate ability to empathize with my mother. I wanted her to be happy again. That meeting in the hotel was a milestone in my life. I had connected with my mother in a way that was beyond description. Not many words were spoken, but the emotional exchange was profound. I saw vulnerability in her that I had never witnessed. I wanted to make it right. I wanted her to know that things would be OK. In some way I felt responsible for her happiness.

A few days after that meeting with my mom, my step dad sent my brothers and me to live with my real father. He lived an hour away in Orangeburg, South Carolina. I did not want to leave my mother, but was forced into it.

CHAPTER 2

ADOLESCENCE

The scene in Orangeburg was an uncomfortable one to say the least. My father had been remarried for several years and had a stepson and another biological child with his new wife. I think my half-brother, at that time was around four years old. From the get-go, I felt like an intruder in their "family." We never discussed anything, but you could feel the tension. My father had purchased a used mobile home to put out back for his new addition to his current family. It was a weird time. We were enrolled in eighth grade in Orangeburg, and I felt like the proverbial fish out of water. I knew no one. We were triplets, and that made it slightly difficult to blend in to our new surroundings. The entire episode is really a blur and not a very happy memory. I do remember being bullied by some kid who said he was going to beat me up. It was about that same time that I told my dad I wanted to go back to Sumter to be with my mother. His feelings were mixed. In my mind, I would be one less burden on him. A few days later, I packed all my belongings into two white trash bags and boarded a Greyhound bus for the trip home. I was excited, but I also did not know what to expect when I arrived in Sumter. It was a Saturday evening, and my mom and Bruce picked me up at the bus station. We drove the short distance back home, to where everything, in the previous months had taken place. The house was a shadow of what I had expected. Bruce had moved his mother in, and the mood seemed somber and heavy. One of my strongest recollections of that day was of walking into the bathroom and noticing that the soap that they were using was some crappy generic brand that we had never used. Our soap of choice had always been Dial. This observation, in my mind, was indicative of what my mom's life had been reduced to: a cheap, flimsy, artificial imitation of the real thing.

The next day, a Sunday, I woke up early and went over to a friend's house. Later in the day, I called back home just to check in. Bruce answered the phone, and I asked to speak with my mom. He said she wasn't there. I asked where she was and he responded, "I beat the hell out of her and she's probably at the hospital." I could not believe what I was hearing. I immediately rushed home to find him there. Her purse and all its contents had been scattered throughout the backyard. I quickly grabbed up everything and ran up to Tuomey Hospital in search of her. My heart and mind raced. What would I see? What kind of condition, would I find her in?

At the hospital I peered into the glass window of the ER door. There in the hallway, I saw my mother in a wheelchair with her face cradled in her hands. I was paralyzed. As I entered through the door, she looked up at me and her face was swollen and badly bruised. Bruce had, in fact, "beaten the hell out of her." All I knew to do at that moment was to be there by her side. I had to try and be a man in this thirteen-year-old's body. The helplessness that I felt was insurmountable. Her beating had been my beating. Her pain felt like my own. The question again raced through my mind, why does she stay with this son of a bitch of a man? She told the hospital staff that she had fallen. I felt certain that they knew what really happened.

After several hours we left the hospital in a cab. My mother did not drive. She had never gotten her license in the United States. We went to Mrs. Scott's house which was now in another part of town. The only thing I knew to do was to call the pastor of our church. He came over and talked with my mom for quite some time trying to give her counseling and helpful advice. A day or so later, she and I were out trying to find a place to live. I remember specifically going to one older lady's home who had an apartment attached to her house. After viewing the apartment, I remember begging my mom to take it. It's a place to live, I thought, anything, just to get away from Bruce. There was something about the apartment that she did not like. Maybe it was the fact that the older woman would know our business. My mom chose to pass. I had heard of a house that a friend of mine was moving out of and really liked the place. It had been a second home to me in previous years. A few days later, we moved into that house at 415 N. Magnolia

St. We had done it. We had gotten away. We were safe.

A few weeks into our new home and new life, Bruce started coming around again to visit my mother. I was angry and I thought to myself, why is she allowing this? I felt that we had made an agreement to start over, and now he was spending the night. They would sleep together, and then she would not see him for several days. I was confused, but we never did talk about it. Luckily, Bruce did gradually fade away and disappeared from our lives.

During this very transitional time, I had entered the eighth grade, at Bates Middle School. It was a strange time. I certainly was not focused on school work, and had my behavioral problems. I would cut school frequently. Perhaps I was acting out the turmoil that I felt within. The times that I did do things that were wrong, I would immediately feel guilty. I knew it was not right. I did get caught on one occasion for cutting class. My mom found out and I felt as if I had let her down. She and I had a heart to heart, and I promised that I would do all I could to make life as easy as possible for her. I believe that it was the first time in my thirteen years of life that she and I were able to relate on an adult level.

The summer following my eighth-grade year, which I had somehow passed, my brother Matthew had decided that he wanted to come back to Sumter to live with us. I had mixed feelings and emotions. By this time, I had grown accustomed to being an only child and I reveled in it. Now he was going to change all that. He did move back, and it was a relatively easy integration. We both got paper routes delivering *The Daily Item* to make our own money, buy our own clothes and things. We did this to ease the burden on mom, who was only making minimum wage. Plus, my father had her sign a document stating that she would not ask for child support for either of us. As if the forty dollars per week, for four kids that she had received in previous years had made that much of a difference. I must say, to my mother's credit, one of the most solid traits that she instilled within us was an excellent work ethic. It serves me well to this very day and is one of the reasons that this book is now a reality.

Entering Sumter High School in 1982 was unsettling. I felt awkward, with no sense of self-esteem or self-validation. It was also during this time that I had my first gay experience. I had just entered ninth grade. There was this guy named Clifton. He was seventeen. Whenever I saw him, he would make obvious eye contact and be extremely friendly. This went on for several weeks. Of course, I thought he was beautiful. He used to play football and was well developed for his age. He was very handsome to say the least. He was three years older and completely mysterious. I kept wondering why he was going out of his way to have anything to do with me. I did not think I was attractive and was missing a front tooth which made me even more self-conscious.

One day after finishing my paper route, I found him at my house. He had driven over in a green Jaguar. I was stunned and elated. Since our first meeting, I had come to realize that I had a crush on him, but was completely oblivious to what his feelings or intent was for me. I had noticed pictures of girls in his wallet and just assumed that he was a really nice, straight guy. I remember the feeling of wonder, giddiness, and amazement that I would experience talking with him. There was a sense of excitement and adrenaline that I had never felt before, and yet, I felt safe.

A few weeks later, during Christmas break, we went to a movie. And later that evening it happened, my first gay experience. I was fourteen. I felt immense guilt afterward. I had been taught in church that it was immoral and sinful before God. On Sunday mornings, after the worship service, I would do the obligatory walk forward and ask the pastor to pray for me, although I did not give specifics as to why. This whole cycle continued for several months. I would try to stay away from this person and would do well for a while, but then it would happen again.

About this same time, my mom met a wonderful, kind man named Larry. They had been introduced at church, and there was an instant and obvious attraction. I saw my mom happy again for the first time in many years. There was a zeal and enthusiasm in her that I had seldom witnessed. They dated for several months, and then married. To give you an idea of Larry's character, he spoke with Matthew and me about his intent to marry mom and asked for our blessing. We were more than happy to give it. Larry truly was a gift from above. He, like my mother, had been divorced twice and had endured his own difficulties. They were good for each other and we were a family again.

After they married, we moved across town to a new home and a new beginning. This distance made it difficult for me to visit Clifton and, eventually, we stopped seeing one another. The last I heard he was in some trouble with the police for breaking and entering and drugs. Over the years, I gave his stepfather a call just to find out about him. I often wonder where he lives now and what he might be like today. I am curious as to what kind of man he turned out to be.

CHAPTER 3

A CALL TO MINISTRY

During this time, I became involved with church sponsored speaker's tournaments. For two years, I made it to state level. I excelled at and enjoyed the practice and the competitions. At the age of sixteen, I began to feel a calling to ministry. I truly believe it was genuine, and I also believe that it was a sort of appeasement for my "homosexual sin." We had always attended summer camp. It was an intense emotional high of being around others who had the same Christian beliefs. There was a sense of community. There was great music, powerful services, fun activities, and newfound friends. Coming home from that type of experience was always difficult for me. I often wished that the feeling would linger forever. Wouldn't life be great? I would spend an entire week on this emotional high and then have to come back home to the real world. I would be depressed for several days afterward.

The thing about sex and the church that really confused and pissed me off was the fact that no one would ever address it. No one would come out and say that sexuality is normal and God-given, much

less homosexuality. Because of this, I had always felt
that sex was something lewd and shameful. Even to
masturbate, which is completely natural as a physical
being, made me feel like I had failed, regarding what
I was taught. I felt somehow lacking for giving in to
these natural urges. One year at camp, I even lied on
a survey about the topic of masturbation and whether
I did it or not. The minister who ran the camp later
came up to me and asked point-blank, if I had been
truthful in my responses. I thought to myself, what
business was it of his? He had never spoken about the
topic of sex in an affirmative manner. No one in my
life had. What audacity on his part. I feel quite
certain that their questionnaire was not as confiden-
tial and private a survey as they had led us to believe.
Needless to say, my notion of sexuality in general,
was not a positive one.

After high school, I entered North Greenville
College, in Tigerville, South Carolina. At that
time, it was a two-year, Liberal Arts College. It was
small and conservative with very strong Southern
Baptist ties. I had enrolled as a Religion major. I
began to blossom and come out of my shell, involved
in every possible organization on campus. I even led
revival teams that would go to various churches
throughout the state. We would host Bible studies and
fellowships throughout the weekend and then
conduct the Sunday morning worship service. I
usually did the sermon. I got most of my speaking
experience this way. It was a time of great personal

validation and self-esteem building. A close and dear female friend and I still refer to those two years as grades 13 and 14. I also had the opportunity to serve as a chaplain for two summers at Table Rock State Park. These were all very positive and nurturing experiences. It was what I needed at that point in my life.

I graduated from North Greenville College in May of 1988 with an Associate of Arts Degree in Religion. I transferred to Gardner-Webb College in Boiling Springs, North Carolina, to finish out my Bachelor of Arts Degree in Religion. It too was a very positive experience. I was Mr. BSU (Baptist Student Union) this and Mr. FCA (Fellowship of Christian Athletes) that. As I reflect on my college experience now, I was probably, in all honesty, very unapproachable. Sadly, if you were not involved in the BSU or the like, and did not fit the traditional idea of what a Christian was supposed to be, then I had no use for you. Like some sort of unofficial "God Squad" or "God Patrol." I now look back at myself and laugh at this arrogance. What ignorance and short sidedness. Definitely a regret and the reason that I am today accepting of those who are different. In fact, I welcome diversity. I celebrate it. I revel in it.

In the fall of 1987, I had just entered my sophomore year at North Greenville. My attention was caught by an incoming freshman named Anna. We met at a visitor's day for potential students. I was a campus ambassador and responsible for giving tours and talking about the school from a student's perspective. I was drawn to her in that brief encounter. There was something about her that caused me to take notice. She was adorable, effervescent, and so full of enthusiasm. There was a fire and vitality for life in her eyes. This was immediately noticeable to me. Perhaps I saw part of myself reflected in her. Whatever it was, it made quite an impression. We spent more time together, and with each interaction, she became even more attractive to me. She was the real deal. There was nothing artificial or shallow about her. Her dad had been a minister for many years. This excited me. She knew, firsthand, what life was like in this profession. She was the only girl in her family and had three brothers, two of whom were older and one younger. A few months into this friendship, I asked if she would like to start dating. She accepted. How did I get so lucky to meet someone so amazing? I had dated other girls while in high school, but no one had ever had such an impact as Anna did. She was truly genuine and a very remarkable person. I saw in her an equal, a future companion, wife, mother, and partner in the ministry. In my mind, she was the perfect ideal of what a preacher's wife should be.

Over the next few years she taught me how to enjoy life; both the good and the bad. She knew how to make me laugh. Her sense of humor, quick wit, and unmistakable smile are impressed on my memory. We had fun and really did enjoy each other's company. Her family was my own. Anna's parents, particularly her mother, were very good to me. They had such a positive impact on my life that it still touches me to this very day. In September of 1989, while at Gardner-Webb, I asked Anna to marry me. I had given her a ring and we became engaged. She was a junior majoring in Education and I was a senior. Her parents wanted her to finish her education before we got married, and rightly so. Late August of 1990, as she was about to begin her final year of college, I headed off to seminary.

CHAPTER 4

AN ATTEMPT AT MARRIAGE

With two hundred dollars in my pocket, and all my worldly possessions, I set out for New Orleans Baptist Theological Seminary. I basically entered the seminary, because a college professor had told me that if I was going to work in a church, I needed to have a seminary degree. That made sense to me, so off I went. My experience there was a complete eye-opener. I went from being in a predominantly Southern Baptist area into Roman Catholic territory. Baptists in "The Big Easy" were small in numbers. I had now become the minority. It was my turn to be on the outside looking in. I must say that it was the most important and the most profound lesson of my two years of seminary attendance. That experience took me out of my comfort zone and forced me to look at the bigger picture.

In addition to being a full-time seminary student, I was also working two and three jobs to make money to live on. I drove a school bus, worked in a professor's office, and at a nearby church. I never really had the luxury of having someone to fall back on financially. It just was not an option that was available to me. I had put myself through college and now had this same responsibility for this part of my educational quest.

By most accounts, I was probably considered somewhat irreverent by my fellow classmates. I would joke with professors and try to lighten the mood, but many of the other students were way too serious. Things began to change for me. I had graduated from Gardner-Webb, which was considered to be a very liberal college and had now entered the most conservative Baptist seminary. This scenario would foster the biggest and most traumatic events of my life.

Most people would jokingly ask what a Baptist Seminary was doing in New Orleans of all places. I would respond lightly, "I guess they wanted to go where it was most needed?" If you've ever been there, you know that the city is very open and most anything goes. It was commonplace to see gay guys in the French quarter. I was now twenty-two years old, and the urges that I had repressed since the age of fourteen started to find their way back to the surface. Once again, the immense guilt and confusion set in. I would ask myself, "How can this be? How is this possible?" I'm in seminary for God's sake. I'm on the staff at a local church. And to make matters even more complicated, I was engaged to be married.

The wedding date had been set for several months. We were to be married on Saturday, January 4, 1992, in Anna's small hometown in rural SC. Of course, the service would be held at The First Baptist

Church. My brother Matthew was married a week before. I was the best man in his wedding, and he was the best man in mine. In all honesty and sincerity, I loved Anna, but I knew that I should not be getting married. It just didn't seem right. The Thanksgiving of 1991 was a real low point for me. I had driven back to South Carolina to spend it with her and her family. During the entire twelve-hour drive, I was consumed and riddled with how to call the entire thing off. I knew in my heart that I should not go through with it.

Naturally, all the conversation during the holiday was about the impending wedding and the details surrounding the event. I kept obsessing over how they might react if I spoke my truth. What would they think? Could they handle it? Would I be seen as a disappointment? Would I upset their entire lives? Do I spare their feelings by sacrificing my own? The pressure was unfathomable. There was no way possible that I could hurt them in such a devastating manner. I had such an enormous fear of not wanting to disappoint others that I went against my own will, therefore disappointing myself. I remained silent. I chose not to reveal my true feelings, my heart, if you will. We were married some eight weeks later.

My wedding ceremony, to this day, was more like a movie that was unfolding before me. It felt as if I were viewing it as just another guest in the audience. It did not seem real. One positive aspect of that very surreal day was the fact that I was able to visit with friends and family who were so dear to me. It was a small consolation. Perhaps, even almost enough to validate that I had made the right choice. After all, this is what was expected of me, and so I must do it.

After the reception, my new bride, and I hopped into my white Pontiac 6000, and began our drive to Florida for our honeymoon. Driving down I-95, all I could think about was the fact that I had just made the biggest mistake of my entire life. Our honeymoon night was spent in Jacksonville, Florida, at the Ramada Inn. Awkward does not even begin to describe the scene that evening. Here I was, a twenty-three year old and had never slept with a woman before. I was a nervous wreck. Somehow, I made it through the ordeal.

Like good Southern Baptists, we awoke early the next day and headed to the Sunday morning worship service at First Baptist. As is customary, all visitors were asked to stand and be recognized and welcomed. As I stood there with my new wife, in front of thousands of total strangers, I wondered if anyone could really see the storm that was churning inside of me.

We spent the remainder of our honeymoon in the Bahamas. The resort was beautiful, with several huge whirlpools outside where the water ran down rocks and into them. It was obvious that there were many other honeymooners there as well. They all seemed so happy and in love. This was evident by obvious displays of affection. I knew that I did not have that same desire for my own wife. On one occasion, I sat in the Jacuzzi thinking how romantic this place was. It would be so wonderful to share this intimate setting with a man that I truly loved. There were a few nights when I slept in the other bed separate from my wife. I used the excuse that I did not feel well and was very tired. I was just going through the motions.

During this same time, I was working as the Single's Minister at First Baptist Church of Gulfport, MS. I had found an apartment for us. Each day I would drive one hour to New Orleans to attend class and work at my campus job. I would end the day by driving the hour back to MS. Recalling that period in my life, even now, is painful. It was a time of immense sadness and such a sense of being lost. The only thing that I could concentrate on was the question, what have I done? I recall sitting in a pastoral counseling class during that time and thinking to myself, how can I help other people when I cannot even help myself?

I had finally decided that I would leave. I would move to Atlanta and start a whole new life. In my mind, it was the only way. I first left on Valentine's Day of 1992. Anna was away babysitting at a church member's house to make some extra money. I packed up my stuff at home and drove away. I had roughly two hundred fifty dollars to my name. I headed to Atlanta, spent the night in a hotel just outside the city, and woke up early the next morning, Saturday. As I sat up in bed, the reality and magnitude of the situation hit me. I could not believe what I had done. I was scared, and I called her that afternoon to apologize. I said I was sorry for what I had done and wanted to come home. She took me back.

The second attempt took place just two weeks later. It was pretty much the same scenario. Once I got to Atlanta, I checked into a hotel. I tried to sleep but could not. I kept thinking how can I hurt this beautiful woman in such a horrible way? I have this secret inside about who I really am, but no one must ever know.

I tried to commit suicide twice. The first was by attempting to hang myself in the hotel room with the lamp chord. That failed. I proceeded to write a suicide/apology letter to my wife and dropped it in the mail. I then drove to a mini warehouse and parked the car inside, still running. I pulled the door down, took several Benadryl and waited. In my mind it was the only way. I wanted to drift off to sleep and disappear forever.

After sitting in the car for several hours, I realized that this attempt to end my life had also failed. I drove to a nearby phone and called Anna. I still remember it as if it were yesterday. As I stood outside at the payphone, it was damp, raining, and cold. This day had been the lowest point of my life. Again, I told Anna how sorry I was and wanted to come back home. By this time, all hell had broken loose. All of our family members now knew what I had done, as well as the entire church staff of First Baptist, and probably some of its members. Fear, angst, and dread consumed me for the entire six-hour drive back to Gulfport.

The next morning, Sunday, I was called into a special meeting by the church staff that felt like a precursor to the firing squad. One of the first questions out of a staff member's mouth was, "Do you have homosexual tendencies?" I was completely floored. I hesitated and then said, "Absolutely not. Why would you even ask such a ridiculous question?" I replied. Another staffer stated that I very seldom showed affection to my new wife in public. I responded by saying that I had never really had a strong example of what a solid marriage was supposed to be and that was the reason.

I was allowed to stay on staff if I sought counseling. I said I would and it seemed to appease them. But deep inside, I knew that I had lost their respect, their admiration. This golden boy was now tarnished and serious cracks were beginning to show.

Needless to say, things at home were troublesome. I did my best to console Anna and put her mind at ease. I assured her that the worst was behind us. I thought that perhaps if we moved onto the seminary campus, and were around other newly married couples, things might improve. Somehow, perhaps, I could learn to live this way, to live this lie for her sake. We moved into married housing. The move and all that entails was a brief distraction from what was taking place within me. I even took a third job at The Cornstalk Hotel, working at night, to lessen the financial burden and stay busy.

One moment of crystal clear clarity, during this dark period came while at the top of a building in downtown New Orleans. Myself, Anna, and another newly married couple from seminary were looking out over the city. The night sky was mesmerizing. It held so much promise and potential. At that moment, I got an image of an eagle that innately needed to fly, but was being chained to the ground. The horizon was before him, but still just out of reach. Freedom eluded him. This was my exact sentiment. This visual offered me a glimmer of hope. I could choose to be true to myself or be held captive by fear. My fear was my chain. It was a moment of epiphany.

Shortly thereafter, while working at the hotel one evening, I called a former seminary student who had left school several weeks before under mysterious circumstances. His name was Jason and it was rumored that he was gay. As we spoke candidly, I confided in him about my own truth. I was reaching out for the only lifeline I knew. I was seeking validation that it was safe to be honest about who I really was. I told him of my dilemma and he offered to let me stay with him until I could figure things out. I would end up sleeping on Jason's couch for a month until I found my own place.

〤

CHAPTER 5

PICKING UP THE PIECES

I left for the third and final time, on April 1 of 1992. I knew without a shadow of a doubt that this was it. I could do it and be strong in my decision to follow through with it. It was a decision to follow the truth of my heart. Once again, I loaded up the car and drove away from my life as a husband, a seminary student, and life as I had known it. It was the single most terrifying thing I've ever had to do. I stopped by a barbershop to get a haircut, and then drove to Jason's apartment to lay low. I knew that I had to get some sort of job to make money on which to live. I took a position as a car salesman at Ray Brandt Nissan. I was getting by the only way I knew how, one day at a time.

One of the things that comforted me during this period was work. It kept me busy, and fed my strong work ethic that my mother had given me. My ability to work was the one constant in my life. I found my own apartment on St. Charles Avenue. Ironically, it was just two doors down from The First Baptist Church of New Orleans, where many of the seminary professors and students attended. I was hiding out, but each day I became more confident in the decision to leave my prior life. I sold my car and bought an old VW Fox so I would not be recognized.

One incident during this time, which still remains with me to this day, was a call from my former pastor and "father in the ministry". He had left several previous voice messages, insisting that I call him. On this particular day, his voice message was an ultimatum, telling me to call him or this was it. I never returned his call. How could I at that time? He was the Southern Baptist Denomination personified. I knew his conservative views on homosexuality, and was also aware that he would try to change my mind. And I probably would have gone along with it, just to appease him and make him happy. This was a man who had been more of a father to me than my own dad. I had been a part of his family, and he treated me like his own son. It was largely because of him that I surrendered myself to this call of ministry. I later found out, through my brother, that this experience had been the most difficult thing my ministerial father had ever gone through.

After several weeks of hiding out, I had a visitor at the car dealership one afternoon. A strange man approached me and asked me if I was Mark Hyde. I instinctively knew why he was there. He was a detective that Anna had hired to find me. He informed me that he was actually the second detective that she had hired. The first one had no luck in finding me. We talked for nearly an hour. He told me that I seemed like a really nice guy who was going through a tough time. He let me know that Anna wanted to meet to talk and be assured that I was okay. I agreed to the meeting which took place a few days later. I knew I owed her that much. To keep things civil, we met in Copeland's Restaurant, on St. Charles Ave. The professor that I had worked for on campus accompanied her. I now knew intimately how my mom must have felt the day I met her in the hotel, some eleven years earlier.

I was seated at the table, and they walked in. I stood, hugged her, and shook his hand. We sat down and then she mustered up enough courage to ask me if I was gay. I responded, with heartfelt honesty, that I was but did not know if I could be happy living that way. We talked for several minutes. She told me that it had been a very traumatic time for her. When I disappeared, she did not know if I was dead, had a drug problem, or left her for someone else. Word had gotten out that I had been staying with Jason and the rumor was that I had left her for him. Nothing could have been farther from the truth. I assured her that this was not the case. How could I get involved with someone else when I was struggling to figure things out for myself? She said that she was leaving in a few days to go back to South Carolina. She was moving on with her life.

Anna and I met again a few weeks later, on a subsequent trip back to New Orleans to pick up her last remaining belongings. It was painful to see her. There was such sadness and disappointment in her eyes, but also this immense anger that had started to set in.

Our next contact was a year later, I received divorce papers from her attorney in South Carolina. It was being granted on grounds of a year's separation. I signed and mailed them back that same day. I did call her mom once just to say hello. She was cordial and wished me well. Four years later, I wrote to Anna, asking for the opportunity to openly share some insight into what I was going through back in 1992. She agreed, but under two conditions. The first was that our only correspondence be through mail. And secondly, I had to agree there would be no future contact with her or her family. She said that she had moved on with her life and did not want any kind of relationship with me. This is my letter. . . .

Dear Anna:

I received your letter on August 7, 1997 and completely respect the terms you have requested. I apologize for the delay in my response, but wanted to choose my words carefully, that I might clearly convey the things I needed to share. Please know that this is in no way an attempt at some sort of restoration or plea for forgiveness. I want you to know what I was going through at that time. You have moved on with your life, and so have I. The sad part would have been to do otherwise. I married you in '92, because I loved you. I grew up in the Baptist Church, was educated in its schools, and was headed toward a life of ministry in this institution to which I had become so accustomed. To be married to an incredible young woman with the same goals, religious background, and aspirations was just the perfect manifestation of God's will, in my life. I did everything I thought I was supposed to do that was going to make life rich, full, and meaningful. I went into our marriage with the full intent of spending our remaining years together in ministry to other people. That was genuinely the desire of my heart.

I have always known that I was different. I had my first gay experience in high school at the age of fourteen. Although no one knew, I felt guilty, ashamed, and as if I had let my family down. Can you imagine the untold anxiety and stress? Keep in mind that I was very active in the church, where sexuality was not addressed or talked about, much less homosexuality. From that time forward, I repressed those tendencies. At summer camp, the following year, I started to feel the call into full-time Christian service. Was this an appeasement for what had happened previously, a genuine call, or perhaps a combination of the two? I finished high school, graduated from college, and off to seminary, I went. The feelings that had been repressed for some eight years, started to resurface. How could this be? I had done so well for so long and now at the age of twenty-two, they were emerging. I prayed endlessly and begged God to take them away. I wanted to be "normal."

We were married, and for three months I lived a virtual hell. At the time in my life when I should have been the happiest and on top of the world, I felt completely void and worthless. The drive between Gulfport, Mississippi, and New Orleans was unbearable. I could not focus on school, the two jobs I had at the time, much less on how to be the wonderful, loving, and support-ive husband you deserved. I distinctly remember sitting in a counseling class as they were discussing how to offer guidance to people and thinking how can I help others when I am so confused myself?

There were basically three options I saw at the time. First, I could stay married, pretend everything was fine, and live a complete lie. Keep in mind that this charade may eventually have involved bringing innocent children into this world. Second, I could commit suicide. I did attempt this twice on February 28th and 29th of 1992. This was during the second time I had left. I wrote a suicide note apologizing for the pain and hurt I had caused. I mailed that letter in Atlanta, Georgia, with the full intent of ending it all and keeping secret the real reason for my behavior. I could not bear the thought of letting others down or disappointing them. This seemed to be the only way. I intercepted that letter, just two days later from our mailbox in Gulfport. You never knew. Thirdly, I could walk away, deal with my issues, and try to move on with a productive life. I ultimately chose this option. Please know that I did not leave you for someone else. I gave up my education, new bride, your family, and friends. It was everything that was familiar and comfortable to me. It was everything that defined who I was as a person.

The deciding factor in my decision to finally walk away for good was something I read. It was an article in the February or March '92 edition of the Southern Baptist Courier. The article spoke about the Brotherhood Director of the North Carolina Baptist Convention, and how he had been arrested for attempting to pick up some guy in a public park in Charlotte. Can you imagine the humiliation and embarrassment for this man, his family, and his position of ministry?

The sole purpose of this letter is to open up, and honestly share with you what I was dealing with. We have never talked about it, and I see this as a part of the healing process. Anna, I won't get into trying to convince you that my life as a gay man has made me totally happy and completely content. It has not. But I do have friends, coworkers, and a church that accepts me for who I am. I have had these feelings since the age of three. My real contentment and peace have come through the fact that I have finally been completely honest about who I am. Staying married and living a lie would have been the greatest offense of all.

In closing, please know that I was in no way trying to deceive you. We are taught that marriage is one of the most sacred commitments two people can ever make. I went into our union with that understanding and desperately wanted it to work. You are a beautiful, sensitive, and caring person. If ever I could be married to any woman, it would have been you.

I wish you all the best,

Mark

CHAPTER 6

MY GREATEST ALLY

During the entire seminary exit and coming-out process, I distanced myself from my family. My fear was that they would not understand or accept me. The relationship with my mother was strained to say the least. I remember one incident, a few months after my whole disappearing act that she phoned. There was very little sympathy in her voice and she quickly brought up the subject of money. I had owed my step dad for a small loan. The repayment of that money was the furthest thing from my mind. I was barely surviving. When I needed her support the most, she was emotionally unavailable. She seemed more concerned about the money than my own well-being. Why should I subject myself to that? We would not speak for eight years.

My brother Matthew, who was living in SC at the time, made numerous attempts to stay in touch. I did not know how to respond. What were his motives? Was he trying to change my mind about my decision? Did he know who I really was? Could he deal with it or even accept it? Of all my family, I was only concerned with what he might think. At this point, I had no contact with my other brothers.

Matthew would call and leave messages. It was

never anything threatening or intimidating; just a call to say hello and to let me know that I was in his thoughts. At one point he even drove from South Carolina to New Orleans on Christmas Day that we might spend it together. On that visit, we reminisced about our childhood, fond memories, and our favorite foods from that time. On a few of those nights, I prepared some of those dishes. It was more than comfort food; it was a genuine reconnection on a deeper level in the only way we knew how. We had fun, went to the zoo, and enjoyed each other's company. Not once, did my brother, pressure, interrogate, or demand an explanation about what had taken place several months before. He gave me my space. He was ex-military, had also attended a Southern Baptist college and was quite conservative himself. I knew that the last few months had been difficult for him as well. We had always been so close and a distance had come between us. My brother was reaching out to me by being there. His love for me was evident through his mere presence. I felt no judgment from him, only the concession to let me be where I was at that point in my life.

There were also times when my mother had put him in a position to choose between a relationship with her or me. He chose me. He was truly the only person that had ever stood up for me. I had never taken the opportunity to thank him for his unconditional love during that period. It was a love that sustained me then and still does today. I wrote him this letter at Christmas of 2005, and I would like to share it with you. . . .

Dear Matthew:

Where do I begin to tell you how much you have come to mean to me? I could not imagine not having you in my life. You are and continue to be my greatest source of strength, support, and quiet confidence. It is true, still waters do run deep. I have always wanted to tell you that one of the hardest things I've ever had to do was see you get on that plane in Charleston in 1986 and leave for your military assignment in Turkey. I felt as if a part of me was being taken away. It was then that I truly realized just how strong the bond between us is. Thank you for making the trip to New Orleans in 1992 to spend Christmas Day with me. It was a bright spot in a very dark and difficult time. I know the night you called to tell me that Mom was killed was not easy. I'm glad it was you that gave me the news. I appreciate all you've done concerning that situation since. The many hours spent on the phone and making trips back to South Carolina have not gone unnoticed.

Through the death of Mom and Larry, you were the force that helped us make it through.

Matthew, when I think of the one person in my life who's been my greatest ally, I think of you. Thank you for your tenacity and unwavering love. I admire you for the man, husband, and father that you have become. A friend once asked my idea of the perfect father. I told her that would be you. Not that you don't make mistakes, but that you are willing to admit those mistakes and learn from them. You are a very compassionate, giving, and sincere person. I well up with such pride when I see you interact with Chloe. She's so fortunate to have you as her dad. Your big heart and sensitive spirit cause me to stand in awe. I don't say it often enough, but I believe in you. I consider it a real privilege to call you my brother and my friend.

Love,

Mark

CHAPTER 7

PERSIST

The next few years were a time of learning and growth. My biggest concern was how do I go about making friends in the gay community? I knew how to make friends but the whole gay slant was a different animal. My first actual date with another man was a surreal experience. He asked me out, and I said yes. He was a great person, and we bonded immediately. It was not unlike dates that I had been on as a straight man with a woman. This time, my suitor just happened to be of the same sex. I truly feel that God was looking out for me when he brought Marlon into my life. He was genuine, honest, kind, and well educated. These were the same traits that I had found attractive in Anna. Things might have worked out long-term, but he had to move away with his job. I still consider him a dear friend to this day.

During this time, I also came across many other gay men that came from very similar backgrounds as my own. I would often ask how their transition, from conservative religion to being openly gay, was going. It was an enormous source of comfort to know that I was not alone. I would periodically see some of my former seminary classmates out and about. We would sort of look at each other, and there was this unspoken message, "I too, am trying to figure this all out."

One incident that took place a few months after I left seminary, was a sighting of a former classmate who had to be in his mid- to late-fifties. He was a father and a grandfather. I would see him cruising the French Quarter, school parking sticker and all, in his late model Cadillac. It was blatantly obvious what he was up to. I felt such a huge sense of sadness, sympathy and pity for him. What his life must be like and how emotionally draining it must be to live in these two very different worlds. "There, but by the grace of God go I." It was also a validation of sorts for the choice that I had ultimately made. It was the choice to be who I was. I could not live a lie, especially to myself. I had taken a chance and was grateful I did.

There were some disappointing relationships and I quickly learned that this life can be very superficial. There were instances along the way, where I questioned whether I could be truly happy. I went so far as to contact a former Methodist minister who had previously struggled with this same issue. While in college, I had read his article in <u>Christianity Today</u>. He was now married, living in NJ, and professing an ex-gay lifestyle. He counseled me via phone for a few weeks. I was not completely convinced about his own happiness as an "ex-gay." This had been just another example of my looking outside of myself for my own answers, when I should have been looking within.

At one point, I contacted a former religion professor of mine who I had admired and deeply respected. I brought her up to speed on things and the events that had transpired in the previous months. She had known Anna and may have even had her in some of her classes. I asked my professor with all the sincerity that I knew how to muster, "Can two gay men be happy in a monogamous relationship?" This was another example of my reaching out to the only lifeline I knew. She responded with an emphatic and absolute "Yes." There was no hesitation or doubt in her answer to me. That moment of honesty from a respected mentor put me back on the path of feeling worthy to live my life as a valued human being—sexuality and all. Because of her tenure at a conservative Baptist college, she took a huge risk in answering my question openly. I thank her.

I left New Orleans in February of 1994 and moved to Atlanta, Georgia. I had called my brother one night and tearfully came out to him. I was desperate and very unhappy. I was in a relationship that was not working out, and I wanted to leave the city. My brother and his wife were there the very next day. They packed me up and off to Atlanta we went. It was the new life I had sought. It was a fresh start, a new beginning. I could reinvent myself. Atlanta was good for me. I quickly started making friends, rollerblading at Piedmont Park. I started to exercise on a regular basis and began feeling good about myself. It was during this time that I started to come into my own. I had embarked on the search for myself.

In the summer of 1994, I attended my first gay pride parade. I was nervous and knew not what to expect. I rollerbladed over to view the parade and was amazed at how many other, normal-looking people I saw. It was empowering to know that there were other people like me and even straight people who openly accepted us for who we were. One vivid memory from that day still haunts me. It was a scene that played out on Peachtree Street between two churches. It was the First Baptist Church of Atlanta on one side, and St. Mark's United Methodist Church on the other. St. Mark's had tables set up with water and refreshments; members were inviting us to join them in worship service at any time. First Baptist, which I had attended on several occasions throughout my "former life," had the police out front. Their job was to keep people off the lawn. And of course, in true Baptist fashion, there were picketers with signs that said we were going straight to hell. Which church would you gravitate toward? It was at that moment that I fully realized just how bigoted and elitist a denomination could be. I used to be one of them and now I was on the outside looking in. It saddened me. It frustrated me. It angered me. Who were they to make such a judgment? How could they know my heart and my relationship with God?

From that moment forward, I vowed to always treat others as I wanted to be treated myself. Not to look at their skin color, ethnicity, bank account, etc, but to really look inside and see who they were. It's allowing your human spirit to connect with theirs. What a better world we would inhabit if we truly took this to heart.

Experiences, such as that on Gay Pride, were just another affirmation that this dogma that had become so ingrained in me was not going to help in my search for my own identity. In fact, it would deter it, if given the chance. I had resolved to give up on God, or more correctly, on the limited context in which I had known him.

CHAPTER 8

LOSS

My relationship with God had always been the one constant in my life. As I came to terms with my sexuality, I did not know where I really stood with Him. Was I now going to hell just as the picketers at First Baptist had shouted? After all, it was what I had been taught my entire life. As the years passed, my thinking was, "I'm a good person, I try to live right and treat others fairly." How could God see this and still judge me for being "evil?" I went to church occasionally, but always felt as if I had to conform to the old mentality for the few hours I was there. For ten years I had resolved that my former faith and my current sexual identity could not coexist.

In 2003, I lost my mother in a tragic car accident in SC. She was alone, driving at night, and was hit head-on. It killed her instantly. I was devastated. It was surreal to hear that my mother was no longer alive. A few days later, we had the funeral and pretty much went on autopilot to get through. Once back in Atlanta, the full magnitude started to settle in. The realization that my mother, who I had adored, idolized, and wanted to make proud for so many years, was gone.

My mom's husband, Larry had died in March of 2001 from a heart attack. The several months since his unexpected passing had been very difficult for her. Our relationship had improved and had gotten to a good place. We spent Mother's Day together, just three months before her death. We had a wonderful time and it was a defining moment. I had called several weeks before to say that I was coming to visit and wanted to be with her on that special day. The few days preceding Mother's Day, I had toyed with the idea of backing out. Why, I was not sure. I had gone to visit her family in Germany one month before. I had only met them once before, some twenty-five years prior. The visit went well. I was able to reconnect with them for the first time in my life as an adult. Seeing my grandmother, who was now in her early eighties, was like thumbing through a history book of my mom's childhood and past. My grandmother appeared to be strong and quite stoic in nature. My first impression was that she was some-what guarded in our meeting. I marveled as I sat next to her. She was my mother, some twenty years later. Many of the questions that I had and unknowns about my mom's upbringing came into focus. I was so glad that I had made this trip.

One concern I had about visiting my mom on Mother's Day was the question of whether she would be angry or upset about my trip to Germany without her. I brought back some black-and-white photos from her childhood and had them framed as a gift for her. One photo was of my mom and my natural father. In it, she was twenty-three and he was twenty-one. The photo was of their wedding that had taken place at the local courthouse. It was the first time that I had ever seen this picture, and the only reference that I had to their matrimony.

When I arrived at my mom's on the morning of Mother's Day, I struggled with whether or not to hide this particular photo from her. I did not want to reopen any old wounds. I decided that I would show it to her. I was curious at what her response and reaction would be. As I walked into her home, she hugged me. We sat and I was nervous as hell. I was just as tense as I had been as the twelve-year-old during our meeting in the hotel room twenty-two years earlier. This was the first one-on-one that we had in over ten years. What would we talk about? What questions would she ask me? Would she ask if I was gay? Would she say something to ruin the entire day? Would I retaliate and get angry? I was so anxious that I took two Xanex prior to seeing her. She poured a glass of flavored water for me, and we did small talk for a few minutes. I wished her a happy Mother's Day and gave her the gift. She was genuinely appreciative and became teary eyed. She walked up behind me and put her hand on my shoulder. I flinched. What was her motive? Was her gesture sincere, or just for show? About thirty minutes later, we left for church. The service was nice, and I was proud to be there with her on such a significant day. Of course, there was the loudmouth member who, from across the sanctuary, yells the obligatory question of "Are you married, do you have a girlfriend?" Every church has one of these women. It was all I could do to smile, be polite, and kindly respond, "No, still looking."

After the church service, we drove over to some friends of hers to have lunch. We had a great time. It was such a thrill to see my mom enjoying herself and smiling at me. It was the very thing I had wanted for her my entire life. After several hours we drove back to her house. Once there, still sitting in the car, I told my mom that I should be heading back to Atlanta. I had a rental car and wanted to get it back on time. I got out of the car, walked around, and opened her door. We hugged and the emotional dam burst forth. Her embrace felt real and genuine. There was no doubt that she was emotionally present. For the first time in my life, she wasn't holding back. She was letting herself feel. We had reconnected in the most powerful way: soul to soul. I finally had my mother back, and she had her son. She reached out to me and I accepted. I cried the entire three and a half hours back to Atlanta. That was the last time I saw her alive.

Two and a half months later she was killed in a car crash due to no fault of her own. I am so grateful for the Mother's Day that we spent together and for the healing in our relationship that had taken place. I am glad that I did not back out of that visit at the last minute. That one day had changed my life forever. It also taught me to take the time to tell the people in my life that I love them. To let them know that they are appreciated, valued, and irreplaceable. Don't hold back in showing your love to others.

As an adult, you look back over your life and start

to notice what a tremendous task your parent(s) had in raising you. You come to realize just how monumental a job this can be. I am blown away at my mother's continuance and her ability to endure even during the most difficult of circumstances. There had been times in the past where she let her anger get the best of her and she became physically abusive. For these episodes, she always seemed to be genuinely sorry and I have been able to forgive her.

In all honesty, I would have to say that my mom was one of the kindest and most giving people I have ever known. Many times it seemed easier for her to reach out to other people than to her own children. On the very night she died, I was having dinner with two friends in Atlanta. It was around 9:15 that I distinctly remember telling them, "You inconvenience yourself for your family, friends, and people you care about. You go out of your way to help them." I see this as my mother's legacy to me. Two hours later, I got the call from my brother Matthew that she had been killed.

Some of my fondest memories of her are our Saturday mornings. I was around eight or nine when she and I would walk to downtown Sumter, browse around, shop at McClellan's and Edwards's Department Store, and then have lunch at Kutrate Drugstore on Main Street. There was a small restaurant in the back and we would order grilled cheese sandwiches and tomato soup. We sat, ate, and enjoyed each other's company. During those special times, in my little eyes, all was right and good with the world. On our way back home, we would stop in at the Sumter Bakery for some treats to take home. My favorites were the devil's food cake with white icing and topped with a single cherry.

One thing in my life that I know to be true: treat others with respect and kindness. I learned this from her. In spite of all her apparent flaws—and we all have them—my mother was extremely polite, nonjudgmental, and courteous. I take pride in carrying these very same traits with me to this day. I never had the opportunity to tell her goodbye and to let her know that she did a wonderful job in raising her children. I'd like to take that opportunity now....

Dear Mama:

I never had the chance to tell you how much I cherished and adored you. As a little boy, I thought that you were the most beautiful woman in the world. My favorite picture of you in the pink dress still sits on my desk. I hold it dear because in it you are smiling and happy and that gives me great joy.

I miss seeing you get ready for church on Sunday mornings, and the smell of pot roast that emanated throughout the house. I still laugh at the time you reached for the wrong can and sprayed your hair with Lysol instead of hairspray. I miss the way your purse would smell of Wrigley's Spearmint gum, and how your eyes sparkled and your smile would warm my heart. I miss the times during high school that I would drive you to work at 4 a.m. Those moments together were filled with tranquility, peace, and calm. I still feel your presence and your spirit, especially in the early morning hours. I miss you most in the simple times. I know that even now, you watch over me. I feel so empowered knowing that I have you on my side.

I thank you for making me so independent at an early age. Because of your having me translate your cards, letters, and thank you notes, I now enjoy writing. I appreciate your having me do the grocery shopping for it is now one of my favorite hobbies and I know how to find a great deal. Thank you for instilling in me a strong work ethic and requiring me to treat others with respect and kindness. Your genuine, benevolent, and giving spirit lives on in me. I am grateful for your showing me how to give of my heart; how to make a difference in this world.

Throughout life, I witnessed your pain and sadness. Many times it felt as if it were my own. I wanted to make it better for you. You are now in a wonderful place and can no longer hurt or be disappointed. It is because of this fact that I am able to let you go. I admire you for never giving up even when life dealt you so many tough blows. There were times of great sorrow, challenge, and despair, but you persisted. You were a fighter and indeed a truly remarkable woman. "May God watch between you and me when we are absent one from the other." (Genesis 31:49)

I hope I make you proud,

Your son, Mark

CHAPTER 9

MY WAY BACK HOME

For several years after coming out, I had resolved to leave my former religion in the past. If it could not accept me then I would not accept it. I had to walk away from my Southern Baptist heritage for my own sanity. Would I be forced to walk away from my spirituality as well?

In all honesty, I had "run on empty" for some ten-plus years. I wanted nothing to do with organized religion of any sort. If it reeked of formalized denomination, then I wanted no part of it. There were the random visits to the more accepting churches on Easter and Christmas, but definitely no huge commitment on my part. I had longed for something more personal, genuine, and authentic; something more real.

One morning, a few months after 9/11 with all of its anxiety, distress, and worry, I awoke with the most indescribable calm I had ever experienced. I had awakened from a dream about my own demise and realized that I had nothing to fear. Even today, recollecting that morning still brings me to tears. I had finally realized that I am spirit and death is the ultimate release. I am much more than the trappings of this physical body or earthly world. I was not here to be perfect or tap dance my way through life. I was here to learn how to love, value, and appreciate myself. I was here to discover and own my truth.

Then in 2003, with the loss of my mother, and some other personal tragedies, I felt the need to look deep within. If there was a God who was loving and compassionate, I needed Him in the worst way. Perhaps the events of that year were a wake-up call. An opportunity for Him to say, "I am here. I have always been here. I created you. I love and accept you for who you are. Stop trying to fit in. You are much greater than that." Gandhi was once quoted as saying, "Intellect takes us along in the battle of life to a certain limit, but at the crucial moment it fails us. Faith transcends reason. It is when the horizon is the darkest and human reason is beaten down to the ground that faith shines brightest and comes to our rescue."

I began reading books on life after death, spirituality, and metaphysics from authors such as Deepak Chopra, Wayne Dyer, and Sanaya Roman. One of the books that had the greatest and most profound affects on my life was *Your Sacred Self*, by Dr. Wayne Dyer. It revolutionized my life and gave me back my validity as a spiritual being. It reminded me that I was in fact, a beautiful, unique, and divine creation of God. A "spiritual liberation" of sorts, had begun to take place. One of the quotes from the book that still resonates with me reads, "Authentic freedom is actually the freedom of knowing who you are, why you are here, your purpose in life and where you are going when you leave here."

As I started to wake from my ten-year "slumber," it was as if the universe was sending me signs saying "Welcome back, I have missed you." Another pivotal moment took place one unsuspecting afternoon, when I drove around Atlanta to various theaters trying to find a movie that had a convenient time and was about to start. I did not want to wait for more than fifteen minutes or so. After hitting two theaters with no luck, I headed to the Promenade Theater in midtown. I scanned the marquee and was in luck. A movie was starting in ten minutes. I had heard the title previously, but knew very little about the movie itself. I purchased my ticket and proceeded inside.

As I entered the room where that particular movie was showing, a woman was headed out, who had just seen it herself. I wanted to know what she thought. After a few minutes of conversation, I proceeded to my seat. The movie began, and in a sense, so did my new life in spirit. The movie was entitled, *What the Bleep Do We Know!?*, and it impacted me like nothing else had done before. During the film, I was brought to tears. I thought to myself, this is what I've been searching for. It all makes sense now. That was a Friday afternoon. I was back at the theater, four hours later with my best friend, who, I insisted, needed to see this as well. The movie had an even greater effect on me the second showing. I've seen the movie seven times now, and own two copies. It explores the principles of quantum physics, and how each of us is personally responsible for our own happiness. I highly recommend this movie.

Metaphysics gave me back my life and my spirituality. It met me where I was. A visual to help illustrate this point would be of trying to pour sugar from a fifty-pound bag and attempting to filter it through a very tiny funnel. Remove the funnel, and let the sugar flow forth, as it was meant to. The tiny funnel for me had been organized religion. My Southern Baptist heritage had played a vital part in my early life, but it had served its purpose. "Why go through the operator when you can dial direct?" In my evolution as a person and as a spirit, I now embrace a wider, more expansive concept of God. It is more beautiful than I ever thought possible. It surrounds me. It beckons me. It sustains me.

After seeing the movie, it was all I could do to get my hands on books and reading materials that would encourage me on this new path of self-discovery. A whole new world opened up for me. I started asking God to bring people into my life that would assist and support me in this new growth. I feel as if I had been reborn. I am motivated, excited, and empowered about life in a way that I have not been in many years.

𝕏

CHAPTER 10

———

MEDITATION

A friend of mine, who is quite intuitive, gave me some of the best advice that I've ever been given. She told me I needed to quiet the mind chatter. She was so right. I needed to be silent, listen, and go within. I had always been a very high-energy and anxious person. While in college and seminary, I had been faithful in my daily devotional and prayer time, so I knew the benefits of getting quiet and going within. I found an excellent meditation teacher who taught me the basics. This practice gave me back my sanity. It put me back in the driver's seat. Meditation, for me, is like throwing my anchor out on the sea of life. It grounds, calms, and renews me like nothing else can. Once I began to get quiet, I was able to differentiate between what were my fears and anxieties and what were those of others that I had picked up along the way. As I look back over my life, I was literally a psychic sponge. I would easily pick up the feelings of other people, and most times they were worse than my own. I believe that one of the best and most beneficial things a person can do for themselves is to start the practice of meditation. It will give you clarity and confidence even in the midst of turmoil. When in doubt, go within.

Some of my favorite quotes regarding meditation include:

> Be transformed by the renewing of your minds.
> (Romans 12: 2)

> Be still and know that I am God.
> (Psalm 46:10)

> My mouth shall speak of wisdom; and the meditation of my heart shall be of understanding.
> (Psalm 49:3)

> Give ear to my words, oh Lord, consider my meditation, and hearken unto the voice of my cries, my King and my God. For unto thee will I pray and my voice shall thou hear in the morning. Oh, Lord, in the morning, will I direct my prayer.
> (Psalm 5:1-3)

Deepak Chopra, in *Soul of Healing*, spoke about the importance of meditating. He said,

> To be able to think is remarkable. To be able to not to think is extraordinary.

This quote by Thomas R. Kelly, in *A Testament of Devotion*, illustrates this point beautifully.

"Strained by the very mad pace of our daily outer burdens, we are further strained by an inward uneasiness because we have hints that there is a way of life vastly richer and deeper than all this hurried existence, a life of unhurried serenity and peace and power. If only we could slip over into that center! If only we could find the silence, which is the source of sound!"

When given the advice to clear the mind chatter, I did not realize at that point just how much chatter there really was. Over time, you get used to all the noise, and it becomes second nature. It becomes a way of life. I started looking for someone to show me how to meditate. I wanted someone who had done it for quite some time, and knew the benefits firsthand. I was fortunate enough to read an article in a local holistic magazine about meditation and the positive advantages of such a practice. The article was enlightening and encouraging. I contacted the woman who had written it and signed up for her meditation class.

The class met once a week for an hour for a month. She started with the basics of proper breathing and getting in touch with your breath. She mentioned that most people are so used to shallow breathing that to learn to breathe correctly would take practice. I was indeed one of those people. With each week, we would build on the previous exercise. From starting with proper breathing and relaxation, we proceeded to toning and then concluded with a mantra. In the final class we put it all together, and it was powerful. Never had I experienced anything quite like this and I was hooked. I was now a believer in the power of meditation, and how it can transform your entire life. My first full year of meditation was more helpful than my previous seven years on antidepressants. I learned more about myself, my irrational fears, and the negative family traits that had been handed down to me on a psychological level. They began to disappear. These were learned worries about life, its difficulties, and how disappointing it could all be.

In the last several years, most national news magazines, including Time and Newsweek have published articles on the mind-body connection and the important role of meditation in that connection. I feel very fortunate to have found such a wonderful teacher, who had been studying meditation for thirty years. She prided herself on demystifying the art of meditation and taught it in a way that was simple, and yet profound. I also appreciate the fact that she had no particular religious affiliation, while teaching the class. That is the wonderful aspect of meditation; you can incorporate it into any spiritual belief system. The class was revolutionary for me. I have referred many friends, since, who have benefitted as well.

The adage is so true. "When the student is ready, the teacher will appear." I still consider my meditation teacher to be one of my spiritual mentors. I also consider her a dear friend. I thank you, Linda Miller.

Meditation is the process of finding and listening to the deep stillness within. It is a time when we turn off the noise of the mind's endless debate with itself and listen to the silence. That reconnection with silence nurtures the body, the mind, and the spirit. In this stillness, we recharge the spirit and mind. It is going within to rekindle our inner spark. Some of the benefits of meditation include:

- Stress release
- Calmness and inner quiet
- Decreased anxiety levels
- Reduced negativity
- Focused concentration
- Increased energy
- Helps you to learn to be in the moment
- Freedom
- Boosts the immune system
- Reduced stress
- Decreased depression
- Increased creativity
- Develop intuition
- Relieves headaches
- Reduced blood pressure
- Overcome insomnia
- Greater inner peace and emotional balance

Would you ride a rollercoaster without using the safety bar to hold you in? Meditation is as crucial in finding inner calm on this ride called life. A daily practice of meditation, even if for just ten to fifteen minutes a day can be profound. To find a good meditation teacher or class I would suggest contacting your local Whole Foods store, metaphysical bookstore, yoga studio, or Yellow Pages. My preference is to meditate first thing in the morning. It truly sets the tone for my entire day. Making it a priority, meditation can be one of the best practices we engage in on our path of self-discovery. Try it for yourself. There are many excellent teachers out there who have been doing it for years. They delight in sharing this practice of quieting the mind.

CHAPTER 11

COMING OUT AS A HUMAN BEING

After the ten years since my coming out as a gay man, I realized that I had not come out as a human being. I had always found my validation and purpose in service to other people. I always gave of myself. Quite often, I was like a leaf in the wind. I ultimately decided to take my life back and stop giving my power to someone else. I was a second-class citizen no more. I realized that even as a gay, divorced man who had made numerous mistakes throughout my life, I still had immense value and worth as a person. We are all here for a purpose. It is a divinely inspired task that only we can complete. What is your calling? What is your true path? Nicole Kidman, once said in an interview, "It's your path. You have to follow it."

One night, during this transformational period, I was having Thai food at a local restaurant. My fortune cookie, as small and insignificant as it may seem, spoke volumes. It read, "If you follow someone else, you are ignoring your own path." When you make the choice to become more of yourself and find your own way, the universe will send messages in the most fascinating and seemingly coincidental ways.

There are signs that we are indeed on our own path. Don't miss being present in your own life.

Deepak Chopra once said, "Every life is a book of secrets, ready to be opened. The secret of love is to be found nowhere, but within us, along with the secrets of healing, compassion, faith, and the most elusive secret of all: who we really are."

Growing up as one of a set of triplets, I had always searched for my own identity. I wanted to be an individual, not just one of "the Hyde triplets." I sought those traits that were special and unique to me. Many times, it's easier just to be anonymous and live with the status quo. I wanted something more. I wanted to know my true, authentic self. I love this quote by Oprah Winfrey, "I am ruled by my own heart and my own spirit." It takes courage to be true to oneself. Anything less is a sellout.

Sanaya Roman, in her book, *Personal Power through Awareness*, states "The more you can clear yourself of other people's programs, expectations, and pictures of you, the more powerful you will become." She continues by saying, "Being alone, sitting quietly, allowing yourself to rest physically, emotionally, and mentally will give you an increasingly clear sense of self. In those still times you are not playing out any role or any identity, and your soul can speak to you more clearly. You have the clearest sense of your own energy when you are not around others, when you are alone."

※

CHAPTER 12

MY FRIEND GUS

Inspiration to finally write this book and get it out into the world came when I lost a very dear friend. I had known Gus in New Orleans, and we had dated briefly in 1993. We met through a personal ad that I had placed in the *Times-Picayune*. I was not having much luck, meeting a quality person in the club scene who wanted a relationship as well. I wanted all the same values that a straight, married couple would want in their relationship. I wanted the person to be honest, trustworthy, compassionate, etc. I had met a few people that responded to the ad, but there was not a real connection. Gus called and left a message stating that he liked what my ad said. He was in search of the same characteristics in a relationship.

We agreed to meet one afternoon in front of Tulane University. There was an instant connection. We went to dinner and talked for several hours. Over a period of several months, we became close. At the time, Gus was in medical school. He was one of the brightest people I had ever met. He was Hispanic. His family had migrated to the States from Central America when he was a teenager. At this point, he was still living at home, but did not talk a great deal about his family and I felt they did not know that he was gay. There was also a sense of sadness and discontent in him. When I left New Orleans in '94 for Atlanta, we continued to remain friends in spite of the distance.

On a subsequent visit in 1996, Gus informed me, in tears, that he was newly diagnosed as HIV-positive. This was devastating news and all I wanted to do was make it better for him. Why did this happen to such a wonderful, caring person? I held him and let him know that I would be there for him.

Gus completed his Residency Program in Psychiatry at LSU in 1998. He was excited and found a job nearby and was to start practice in the next few weeks. I spoke with him in early August, and he seemed to be in a hurry to get off the phone. I let him know that he was on my mind, and that I was calling to check in. He apologized for not having time to talk at the moment and assured me that he would give me a call back as soon as he could. I didn't hear from him again.

Several weeks later I was conversing with a friend at the gym who also used to live in New Orleans. I asked if he had spoken with Gus recently? He looked at me with a somewhat surprised expression and said, "You haven't heard?"

I responded, "No, heard what?" He told me Gus was dead. Words do not convey the sadness and sense of loss that I felt at that moment. I immediately left the gym, went home and started making phone calls to New Orleans. I called a few of my old friends, but no one knew anything. I got the idea to call the *Times-Picayune* paper (the same paper through which we met) and did a search for his obituary. I did not know an exact date of death, but the representative searched and searched, and found it. She faxed me a copy. I read it, but was still in complete disbelief.

I didn't have the opportunity to meet Gus's parents, and did not feel that it would be appropriate to call and ask the details of his death. I eventually found out the entire story by calling a former coworker in New Orleans. I had been a physician recruiter in that office and was the one who entered his résumé into their candidate system some four years prior. I remembered Gus saying once that it was my old company that had gotten him his job. The office manager informed me that my dear friend had committed suicide. He died alone and was not found for three days.

I don't believe anything can ever prepare a person to lose someone in this way. The sense of helplessness and total despair he must have felt to do what he did still haunts me. He had mentioned in a previous letter that he had so much to be grateful for, but still felt a deep emptiness within. You see, my friend attempted suicide the previous year and was unsuccessful. It was at that point that he came out to his family about his sexuality and his HIV status. In a situation like this, you ask yourself, what could I have done differently? What if I would have paid closer attention or called more often? Would that have made a difference between his choosing life or ending it? Here was a man who was a trained psychiatrist and yet he still felt that staying in this world was more painful than leaving it.

It is widely believed that at least 10% of the general population is gay or lesbian. The suicide rate for this group is five times higher than the national average. In a study of gay youth, it was found that depression strikes homosexual youth four to five times more often than their non-gay peers.

Gus had so many incredible traits going for him, but still felt no sense of self. I do not know if he ever felt like he fit in, or would be accepted for who he was. I write this book in his memory, and to encourage you, the reader, to see others for who they truly are; unique and beautiful individuals that God created. They are souls that have come to make this world a more colorful, loving, and vibrant place. Instead of ridiculing others because they are different, empathize with them. Embrace them. The ability to empathize and view things from a different perspective other than your own is one of the most powerful tools we can have. When we do this, there is no room for bigotry and hatred. Discrimination would be nonexistent.

To Gus, I miss you my friend. "I thank God upon every remembrance of you." Philippians 1:3.

I think it fitting to conclude this chapter with the following poem:

Does it Matter?

My father asked me if I am gay
I asked does it matter?
He said No not really
I said yes.
He said get out of my life.
I guess it mattered.
My boss asked me if I am gay.
I asked does it matter?
He said No not really
I told him yes.
He said you're fired, faggot
I guess it mattered.
My friend asked me if I am gay
I said does it matter?
He said no not really
I told him yes.
He said don't call me your friend.
I guess it mattered.
My lover asked do you love me?
I asked does it matter?
He said yes.

I told him I love you
He said let me hold you in my arms
For the first time in my life something
matters.
My God asked me do you love yourself?
I said does it matter?
He said YES
I said how can I love myself? I am gay
He said that is the way I made you
Nothing will ever matter again

Anonymous High School Student

CHAPTER 13

LABOR OF LOVE

When I reflect back over the years of my life, there are many special people that took an interest in me for one reason or another. Even in the times that I was most confused and felt completely alone, there were people still rooting for me. Especially in instances where I did or could not believe in myself, others did. I mentioned previously in this book about Mrs. Rosa Scott who was like a grandmother to me. Her reaching out to me and my brothers at the age of six was a selfless act of kindness. That type of generosity of spirit has been a common theme in my life and is unequivocally, the reason I am able to tell my story.

Another person, Mrs. Lucie Anne Eldridge, my music teacher at Bates Middle School, also touched my life in a tremendous way. We attended a concert by Ella Fitzgerald in Columbia, SC once, and I am amazed even today at her insight to expose us to such wonderful and legendary talent. Because of that experience, I now have a deep seated love and appreciation for music and the arts.

Mrs. Eldridge, like Mrs. Scott, was the typical southern, genteel lady. She had a sense of deep compassion and the warmest heart. Although she is a petite framed woman of 5'2", I have always looked up to her. I have the utmost, reverent respect for her, not only as a teacher, but also as a friend. She, too, took an interest in me. Today, she is eighty-seven, and we still communicate often.

On my trips back to South Carolina, I always make it a point to stop in and see her. In early 2000, my partner and I drove to Sumter. It was the day that I had initiated reconciliation with my mom after not speaking for eight years. After visiting with my mom and step dad, I drove to Mrs. Eldridge's home because I wanted Robert to meet her. As we drove up, she and a friend of hers were just about to pull out of the driveway. She got out of her car, came over, and gave me the biggest hug and said it was so good to see me. I introduced her to Robert and she told him it was such a pleasure to meet him. She apologized for not being able to visit at the moment since she had promised to take a friend to a doctor's appointment.

We headed back to Atlanta and a few days later, a letter arrived in the mail from her thanking me for stopping to see her. She wrote that she always enjoyed and looked forward to our visits. She went on to say that it was nice meeting Robert, and I should feel free to bring him anytime. I had never verbally come out to Mrs. Eldridge, but this note conveyed her understanding and acceptance of my relationship with Robert. To me, this speaks of her caliber as a person. She knew that I was a religion major in college, spent time in seminary, and was married briefly. Never once, has she made me feel wrong, inadequate, or any less of a person for being who I am. She is one of the most spiritual people I have ever encountered, and for her to welcome my partner was her acknowledgment that she loved me just the same. I get emotional thinking about her capacity to love me as her own child. If we had more people like her in this world, our lives would be richer for it.

I believe we all need to work to make our lives, a labor of love. What we put out into the world is what comes back to us. If we walk around in life looking for reasons to be angry or offended, that is what we will find. If we go through life seeking opportunities to love, encourage, and uplift, that is what will be given back to us. One of my favorite verses of scripture is Matthew 25:40. It reads, "As you have done it unto the least of these my brethren, you have done it unto me." Each day, I pray for the opportunity to make a difference in this world, ever how small that may be. We grow richer every time we give of ourselves. I encourage you to seek out those same opportunities to lend a helping hand, a kind word, or just a simple smile. It validates the other person and says, "I see you and you are valued." Every person has the right to feel good and positive about themselves. You may very well be the one to change that for them. I firmly believe that when you are having a particularly difficult time in life, this is the best time to do something kind for someone else. It is the greatest pick me up you could ever give yourself. It is true; random acts of kindness will indeed change our world for the better. Be love in action. When you invest in another person's life, the impact is profound and far-reaching. It nurtures their spirit and your own.

It's not about giving or doing because people expect it of you, it's a matter of giving because it comes from the overflow of your spirit and your heart. When we give from this place, it will never run dry. When we give from this place, we not only help in healing others, but we help in healing ourselves as well. The following prayer of Saint Francis contains a powerful message:

Lord, make me an instrument of your peace. Where there is hatred, let me sow love; where there is injury, pardon; where there is doubt, faith. Where there is despair, hope; where there is darkness, light; where there is sadness, joy. O Divine Master, grant that I may not as much seek to be consoled as to console; to be understood as to understand; to be loved as to love. For it is in giving that we are pardoned; it is in dying, that we are born to eternal life.

I am very grateful for all the people that have come into my life and made my telling of this story possible. We all seek a place where we can be safe and truly authentic, a place to drop all pretenses, and just breathe. My favorite line from the movie, *Billy Elliott*, about the little boy that wanted to dance: his teacher told him, 'Always be yourself.'" I so appreciate people like Mrs. Rosa Scott, Mrs. Lucie Eldridge, my brother Matthew, his wife Carla, Robert Manning, Lori and David Guthrie, Bob Bickerstaff, Alan and Dianne Collins of Quantum Think, Leslie Joy, Van Ho, Tonya Owens, Mary Wayne James, and the list goes on. People such as these, have been a beautiful constant in my life. In their company and circle of love, I have found solace and am a better person for having known them. I think it so important to let the people in your life that have been an encouragement and inspiration, know that you appreciate them. Validate their importance to you.

CHAPTER 14

LOVING ME AGAIN

For many years, I felt a need to downplay my happiness and excitement for life. I did this out of fear of not knowing how other people might respond. I remember as a child, seeing my mom in tears and wondering why she was so sad. As a kid, I felt that there was so much in life to be happy about even in spite of a tumultuous home life. I could not understand why she felt the way she did and wanted to make her see life the way I did; through the eyes of a child. Children are naturally happy, and enthusiastic about life. They have not yet "learned" how tough life can be. I think many parents are guilty of squelching that excitement in their children because of their own inability to cope with their difficulties or circumstances.

I have learned in recent years that each of us is responsible for our own happiness. We have a choice each morning, regarding what kind of day it will be. We can wake up and say, "Good God, morning" or we can choose to say, "Good morning, God." The choice is entirely ours as to whether the day will be filled with anger and anxiety or happiness and peace.

One of the most helpful concepts that came out of my seeing, *What the Bleep Do We Know!?* is the premise of "creating my day" which was discussed by Dr. Joseph Dispenza. This principle mesmerized me. I can actually take a few minutes each morning to intend how my day will unfold. It is fascinating, and quite liberating when that kind of power is handed back to you. It is a power that sadly is often taken away when we are children.

For quite some time, especially during the divorce and coming-out process, I lost my joy for life. I believe a lot of it was due to the fact that I was suddenly accepting the status of a minority, a second-class citizen. I was a white male (majority), but because of my being gay, society's message was one of being "less than worthy." There were countless times during this period when I felt as if I wasn't living life, but rather it was living me. To give you a surfing analogy, it was as if I was being pulled under the wave, tumbling along the bottom of the ocean, instead of riding on top of it. I don't believe there is any greater sadness than when one gets to this point. Life just becomes mechanical, mundane, and routine. "A poor player that struts and frets his hour upon the stage and then is heard no more." (Macbeth) I want something more. (Mark)

A dear friend that I have known for some fifteen years is a gay male in his mid-fifties. He also grew up in the Southeast in a very religious home. Both of his parents are now deceased and have been for many years. During conversation about aspects of some gay lifestyles, he made disparaging statements. I asked him point-blank, "Do you think being gay is wrong?"

He responded immediately, "Yes."

My heart sank. It saddened me to know my friend felt this way. He had been a role model for me for many years. I believe that I see for him what he has yet to see for himself. He is one of the most handsome, successful, unique, and creative people I am privileged to know. My friend had lived openly gay for twenty-plus years and still felt, in his own heart, inferior about his sexuality/being. I share the story of my life, specifically, for people like him. Know without a doubt, that you are not a mistake or fluke. You have a purpose and a reason for being here. You do measure up. And you do matter.

I wish I could bring my friend to see that we are each responsible for our own personal happiness. No one but ourselves can give that to us. Not possessions, money, careers, lovers, or friends. It can only come from within. Wayne Dyer once said, "There is no way to happiness, happiness is the way." One of life's biggest challenges is to become comfortable with who we are. It is a matter of accepting ourselves for all the beautiful and good qualities, and also the negative and not so great ones. And we all have them. Many of us go through life being plagued and riddled with guilt for bad choices and decisions that we have made in the past. A better way of looking at these instances is by viewing them as learning experiences and moving on from there with our head held high.

A beautiful quote that helped me reclaim my own spiritual quest is from Teilhard de Chardin, a French geologist, priest and philosopher (1881-1955), it states, "We are not human beings having spiritual experiences, we are spiritual beings having human experiences." Life is our classroom. We will make some bad grades and fail some tests along the way, but it is completely up to each of us if we want to graduate or not. Instead of living in fear and guilt, I encourage you to love yourself again. We are responsible for our own joy in life. Love is much greater than shame. A most inspiring quote about our human potential and making this life count came from Marianne Williamson's book, *A Return to Love*. Nelson Mandela used this very quote during his 1994 Inaugural Speech.

Our deepest fear is not that we are inadequate. Our deepest fear is that we are powerful, beyond measure. It is our light, not our darkness that most frightens us. We ask ourselves, who am I to be brilliant, gorgeous, talented and fabulous? Actually, who are you not to be? You are a child of God. Your playing small doesn't serve the world. There's nothing enlightened about shrinking so that other people won't feel insecure around you. We were born to manifest the glory of God that is within us. It's not just in some of us; it's in everyone. And as we let our own light shine, we unconsciously give other people permission to do the same. As we are liberated from our own fear, our presence automatically liberates others.

I read these very remarkable words on a daily basis.

CHAPTER 15

EACH DAY IS A GIFT

A profound yet simple exercise, that I have done for the last few years, which has had a tremendous impact, is taking a few minutes each day to be in awe. It is as easy as gazing out of a window on a fall day and marveling at the colors of the leaves on the trees. It could be the appreciation of a new flower, budding on a windy, spring day. It could be the wonder we experience as we look into the eyes of a newborn baby or the calm we feel as we walk along the beach. It is about a choice we make to see the beauty in all of life. It is about reveling in the magnificent and the miraculous of this amazing world we inhabit.

One of these moments occured after Christmas of 2005. I was driving back from Asheville, North Carolina, after visiting my brother and his family. It was 6 a.m. and still dark out. As I traveled down I-26, the sky went from being dark and ominous looking to the most beautiful pinks and blues I have ever seen. The sun was rising and the new day before me was filled with endless possibilities and potential. It was completely up to me as to what type of day I wanted it to be. I could choose to follow the old destructive habits that were self-defeating or decide to live up to my full and unlimited potential. I could move through this day with anxiety and fear clouding my every decision, or I could walk in complete joy and harmony with spirit. Even more remarkable was the awareness that each new moment holds the very same breathtaking beauty and incalculable promise, if I chose to see it. . .and I do. As Oprah Winfrey says, "It's moments like these that make you want to go out and do better."

We can find great inspiration in the most simple and ordinary if we choose to see it. We could let every moment fill us with awe. Our world becomes a magical place when we allow ourselves to feel awestruck by it. Living from this place means moving through each day with a smile on our face and a song in our heart. This enables us to experience the wonder in all that we see and hear. Some of the moments where I have felt the closest to God have come during a song, a play, a movie, or the reading of a book. I believe that the arts are one of the most powerful means by which we can become more in tune with spirit. I have such an appreciation for Mrs. Eldridge and people who teach the arts.

Another powerful means of getting in touch with spirit is taking time to express gratitude for the gifts in life. Taking the time to be in a state of thankfulness really does put things in perspective. It calls for us to open our minds and hearts, be in the moment, and just be. It is allowing yourself to be mystified by the things that you once took for granted. Express gratitude for:

- Friends who have loved and supported us through the years
- Family who help to teach patience and the concept of unconditional love
- Pets—the dog or cat that faithfully greets us at the door when we get home— wanting to love and be near us
- Sunny days
- Rainy days
- The seasons of weather
- The seasons of Life
- The teacher who took an interest in us
- The exquisite gift of music
- The gift of laughter
- Random person at the grocery store who smiled just because
- The neighbor who invites us over for dinner at the last minute
- Sunday mornings and the ability to relax, have coffee, and read the newspaper
- Spiritual growth and healing
- The ability to change for the better
- The ability to create the day
- The ability to forgive and be forgiven
- The ability to have compassion for those that are different from us
- A sunrise and its ability to awe and inspire

- A sunset and its ability to captivate and mesmerize
- The majesty of the ocean and its ability to calm our minds and spirits

It's a simple matter of taking time to notice and appreciate the miracles that occur in our lives on a daily basis. We are amazed when we hear of someone who's in a dire situation or facing impending death, and yet they still manage to see the good, beauty, and blessings that exist. It's all a matter of perspective. In those instances, many times, we are brought to tears. We may even feel ashamed for complaining about our petty problems, when a daughter is losing her mother to cancer or a wife knows she will never see her husband again because he was killed in a war. My point is, take the time to be in awe. Make it a habit of expressing gratitude for the gifts in your life. Stand in true wonder and appreciation for how fortunate we are. It truly does put things in perspective. It's the power of being in the moment and fully present. Life flows so much more easily when we live from a state of gratitude and awe. Be aware of every miracle in each moment. Truly look at life, taste life, and embrace life.

With each new day we should seek those opportunities to be our better selves. This choice to be our higher selves is completely ours and it's not about perfection. It's about coming from a place of love rather than envy, hope rather than fear, patience rather than hostility, and acceptance rather than hate.

The following quote by Johann Wolfgang von Goethe, the great German novelist, speaks of this so eloquently. . .

I have come to the frightening conclusion that I am the decisive element. It is my personal approach that creates the climate. It is my daily mood that makes the weather. I possess tremendous power to make life miserable or joyous. I can be a tool of torture or an instrument of inspiration. I can humiliate or humor, hurt or heal. In all situations, it is my response that decides whether a crisis is escalated or de-escalated, and a person is humanized or dehumanized. If we treat people as they are, we make them worse. If we treat people as they ought to be, we help them become what they are capable of becoming.

(Goethe, 1749-1832)

I have a saying, "Make every day a cologne day." We've all purchased that expensive bottle of cologne or perfume and have decided to wear it on special occasions only. Three or four years pass, and we still have the same bottle. Why not decide to make every day an incredible and momentous occasion? There is nothing like the death of a family member or dear friend, to remind us just how fleeting and brief life can be.

Another practice I have incorporated into my life is the act of lighting a single white candle each morning. The lighting of this candle acts as my intent for the day: to bring light into the world. Matthew 5:16, one of my favorite childhood versus, reads "Let your light so shine before men that they may see your good works and glorify your Father which is in heaven." It is remarkable how a single candle, once lit, can pierce the darkness. You can do the same by treating others with love and kindness.

I am fortunate to have people in my life along the way that made unexpected gestures of kindness. I had numerous church families throughout my childhood, college, and seminary experience who treated me as one of their own. Today, I have a capacity to reach out and help others because of the example they set for me.

Each day, make it a priority to go out of your way to show kindness to another. It could be as simple as a smile, a kind word, a helping hand, or a financial gift. One of my favorite acts of kindness is to randomly tell the person in front of me at the grocery store that I want to pay for their groceries. They are usually shocked and in disbelief. It is an act of pure kindness and compassion with no strings attached. I know I have made their day and become a better person for it. It is a beautiful experience and I highly recommend it. We never know how far-reaching a small gesture like this is, but it is infectious.

CHAPTER 16

WHAT'S YOUR STORY?

I had many reasons for wanting to write this book. The whole process has been extremely therapeutic and cathartic. It feels like the right time to tell my story. Even as little as three years ago, I was not capable. I was not ready to own it.

During the "I Can Do It" Conference in Orlando, Florida in October of 2005. I attended an all-day workshop with Sonia Choquette. She is an amazingly gifted woman who has written numerous books on spirituality and intuition. The entire experience was truly astonishing. About an hour before her workshop was to end, she started pointing to people randomly and asking the question, "What's your story?" There were several hundred people in the room, and she immediately pointed to me. I froze. In her *go for it* attitude, she encouraged me to tell my story. I hesitated and then replied, "Do you want the good version or the bad one?" I then went for it. I said, "I'm a former Southern Baptist seminarian and I'm gay." In her effervescent and sincere manner, she responded without missing a beat. She said, "It's a great story, but it's not true." As she continued to call on others in the audience, I pondered her comments. They made total sense.

As contradictory as that statement may seem, in regard to my writing this book, it's absolutely true. I wrote this book hoping to help others along this same path of self-discovery. I have written it and now am ready to let it go that it might encourage those who need to hear its message. Why would I want the rest of my life to be completely defined by those early experiences? Yes, they were a great catalyst to bring me to where I am today, but I am more than my past. And you are more than yours. Why would we reduce our magnificent, wonderful selves to the past alone? Sonia was saying to let go of the ideas and beliefs that no longer serve. Reinvent a new story for yourself.

It can be a frightening and liberating thought when you seriously consider it. If I'm not the kid who struggled with being gay for the first twenty-two years of my life then who am I? If you're not the mother who raised six children and has been married for thirty-five years then who are you? If you're not the doctor's wife who helped put her husband through medical school and was then left for a younger woman then who are you? The answer, we are much greater and more viable than any of that. We are spirit. Let me give you an example. When we board an airplane to fly from say, NYC to LA, we are assigned a seat. We inhabit seat 32A. For that entire flight we are basically reduced to "the passenger in 32A."

Why continue to define ourselves by the different adversities from our past and wear them like a Scarlet Letter? Our potential and value as God's creation is so much greater. We all have a story that others can benefit from, even if it's just in taking courage that they are not alone. Tell your story. Let it be known that you have made it through and then create an even better one for yourself. The rest is still unwritten.

I used to be somewhat angry at the church for not stepping up and saying that sexuality is normal. That it is God-given, beautiful, and nothing to be ashamed of. I used to present the "Ex-Southern Baptist Seminarian" label as a negative. Now that I look back, it is quite a positive in my life. Growing up in the conservative Southern Baptist denomination was actually a stepping stone to where I am today. It served its purpose. I am right where I need to be. I have a greater affinity now for others of different faiths, and welcome diversity of all sorts. I know what it's like to be discriminated against so I guard against doing it to others. What are the experiences in your life that you view as negatives when seen from this perspective, are actually positives?

I challenge you to expand your talents. Try something new. Widen your definition of who you are and how you perceive yourself. Push yourself in ways that you never thought possible. I assure you that you've only scratched the surface of your full potential as a creation of the Divine.

)(

CHAPTER 17

OH, NO!

My natural father was basically a good ole boy from rural North Carolina. He grew up as one of eleven children. When he finished high school, he did what many people did, he entered the military. My dad met my mother while stationed at Ramstein Army Base, near Frankfurt, Germany.

As I mentioned previously, my parents divorced when I was around five years old. I do not remember a lot of the details of that time, or even of my earliest childhood memories. I vaguely remember, perhaps two or three instances, when they seemed to be happy. Those memories, faded and distant, are all I have from their brief marriage.

My mom married her second husband, Bruce, and from that point on, I had no real relationship with my dad. This was probably due in part, to my mom's own insecurities and my dad wanting to move on with his life. We would spend time with him and his new family every few months. They lived an hour away in Orangeburg, South Carolina. And of course, there were the obligatory visits at Christmas. He would pick us up on Friday night and bring us back on Sunday afternoon. There were some instances, when we excitedly waited for him to come and get us, but he would not show up. This type of disappoint-ment for a kid is heartbreaking. And on some deep level, even now, I am still waiting for him to "show up" in my life. I do believe my dad did the best he could at the time. My mom probably did not make things easy, as she still took issue with how the rela-tionship ended even though both were remarried. Needless to say, I had no real bond with my dad. Even on the brief occasion, when I lived with him during my mom's marital problems, I still felt no emotional connection.

After graduating from high school and entering college, I decided it was time to make an effort to get to know him better. I was an adult, and my hope was that we would connect and be able to relate on a level in which we had not done before. As luck would have it, my girlfriend and eventual wife, Anna, grew up twenty minutes from where my dad lived. Whenever she and I made the three and a half hour trip to her parent's home for the weekend, I always made a point to go and visit with him. I guess in some deep way I was seeking his approval. I wanted him to know, that despite my childhood, I had turned out all right. I was the first in our family to attend college. I was a reli-gion major, had a beautiful girlfriend, and planned on making ministry my life.

My dad came to my college graduation. He seemed proud of my accomplishment and his being there meant a lot to me. I left for seminary, and a year and a half later, I was married. Then in 1992, my facade fell apart. I was not perfect. I had issues, and they were big. He and I communicated very little for several years. By this time, both of his parents had died. I had not known them well, either. I wish I had; it still saddens me to have missed out on having them in my life.

In 2000, at the age of thirty-one, something changed. Perhaps, part of it was due to the millennium premise. I started seriously evaluating my life and examined who I was and my level of honesty with my family, particularly my dad. My hair was receding, and instead of trying to disguise it, I cut it very short. It was liberating. I was in essence saying to myself, and the whole world, this is who I am. Take it or leave it. It was so much more than mere hair loss. I was owning up to who I was. I was coming into my own. During this period I reconnected with my mom and her third husband, and that relationship was improving.

In March of 2000, one evening after dinner and a few glasses of red wine, I decided to call my father. He answered the phone, and I began, "Dad, it's Mark. I am at a point in my life where I don't want to have anything to hide. If you have any questions of me that you want answered, feel free to ask." He was taken back, but said that he had no questions at the moment. I responded, "Fair enough," and continued by saying that I had some questions for him and wanted him to be as honest and open as possible. He agreed, and I proceeded to ask how he and my mom met. He told me that he was in a bar one night. They met, ended up sleeping together, and she became pregnant. My dad, being in his early twenties at the time, did the honorable thing and married her. That is the story of how my oldest brother was born. Perhaps I had always suspected as much, but it was so interesting, hearing the story come directly from him. I asked if he loved her. He said he did. I asked what her parents thought. He said my grandfather hated him for getting his daughter pregnant, but my maternal grandmother seemed to like him.

The conversation continued. I asked my dad about Christina, their only daughter, my sister, who died when she was two. I had never heard either of my parents speak of her or how she died. My father began to cry. It had been thirty-three years since her death, and it was still very painful. He explained that Christina had fallen on the outside steps of the house and hit her head. They thought she was okay, but she had a concussion. She died in her sleep. That evening on the phone, I experienced a side of my father that I had never witnessed before.

On subsequent visits, Dad didn't take me up on my offer to answer any questions he might have, and I was okay with that. I figured he would ask when he was ready to hear it. Then in June of 2003, I returned to South Carolina to visit. My half-brother, Stephen, had recently married and my dad wanted me to congratulate them. We spent about thirty minutes with Stephen and his new wife. Seeing them, reminded me of my own marriage attempt eleven years prior. As Dad and I drove the short distance back to his home, he asked me, "Are you seeing anyone?" I was a little surprised, but replied, "No, I've not really met anyone special," throwing it out casually. (I was single at the time.) He then asked,

"Do you think that you will ever get remarried?" Surprised even more, I hesitated and said, ""Uhm?? No, uhm,...probably. . ." I then decided not to go there with the whole song and dance that most gay people get accustomed to when asked such questions. I responded, "Uhm, Dad, uhm. . . I don't know if you know or not. . . But, Uhm. . . I'M GAY!" His immediate response was, "Oh, No!" I just knew at that moment, he was going to run off the road and crash into a tree at sixty miles an hour, because of what I had just announced. I said, "Dad, did you really not know? Come on."

He said, "Well, I thought but maybe. . ."

I told him that I've known since I was a child that I was gay. I had done everything to try to be otherwise, including trying to end my own life. I told him that it was just the luck of the draw. Just as I was born a triplet with green eyes and blond hair, I also happen to be born gay. I said, "Dad, it's taken ME thirty years to be comfortable with it so take as much time as YOU need." In all honesty, it was actually a relief to finally have that conversation. I knew where my dad was coming from. He had just seen his youngest son get married. All of his five sons were married, except for me. I genuinely believe that he was coming from a place of love: that place as a parent wanting their children to be happy and genuinely cared for. I assured him that I had wonderful friends in my life that were like family to me. I wanted him to know I was not some loner that faced a horrible life. "Dad, I've owned who I am, and I'm the happiest and most content that I have ever been."

Coming out to my dad and the fact that we were never terribly close, I felt I had nothing to lose and all to gain. I knew that my self worth as a person was not contingent on his positive or negative response. When I speak with him on the phone or in person, I always say, "I love you." And, although he is a man of very few words, there is an honesty in our relationship now that I believe few men have with their fathers. I am fortunate.

ℵ

CHAPTER 18

NO MAN IS AN ISLAND

My mom's second husband was physically abusive throughout their marriage. It was common place to be awakened at 3 a.m. to the sound of his beating her. As an eight-year-old, to hear your mother beaten and crying out for help, is traumatic. A child feels completely and utterly helpless. A sick feeling of dread and panic grips you and won't let go. The very core of a child's world is shaken. My brothers and I could only lie in bed, in the next room, frozen in fear. At a time, when we most needed a positive role model, he greatly and utterly disappointed. I think somewhere along the way, I decided to be that positive role model for myself.

For many years, I was angry at Bruce and hated him for what he had done, not only to our mother, but to our childhood. I had not seen him for twenty-plus years. The night before my mom was to be buried, he appeared at the funeral home. My brother came over and said, "You'll never believe who just walked in."

"Who," I asked.

"Bruce," my brother replied.

I was completely caught off guard. I did not know that Bruce was still alive. I looked around, but Matthew had to point him out. I was shocked. I did not even recognize this man who had been our step-father for nine years. At that moment, I made a choice. It was a choice to forgive. I walked over, hugged Bruce, and thanked him for coming. Instead of his bulky, stocky build, and cocky demeanor that I remembered, he was a mere shadow of the man who brought terror into our home. I felt sad for him. Life had not been kind to him, just as he had not been kind to our mother.

For decades, I hoped, that in spite of my childhood, to have escaped unscathed and relatively normal. It was not until some time later that I realized, not everyone walks through life in a constant state of anxiety. I wasn't quite sure what this heaviness was; this nervousness that permeated my being. Today, I am completely aware of just how much those childhood experiences affected me and still can. When one grows up in a situation such as this, their ability to cope and deal with the everyday stresses and pressures is significantly impaired. I say all of that to say this: when you need help—and we all do—ask for it.

I often wonder how different life would be had I sought some sort of counseling while struggling with my sexuality. Perhaps I would not have attempted to end my life. I was at the darkest place I had ever encountered and felt completely alone. I wanted someone to help me, but was afraid to ask. I had always felt that asking for help was a sign of defeat, like an admission that I really did not have it all together as much as everyone may have thought or expected. This mentality almost killed me. To seek out assistance when you need it is actually a sign of strength.

I am a huge advocate of therapy. It was a new concept to me to actually sit down and discuss my past, my problems, and their impact. It was frightening to be completely open about what I was feeling. I had never had this luxury as a child. I had to learn to make myself vulnerable again. I initially sought counseling to deal with the issues concerning my mother. Therapy allowed me to bridge the gap of eight years of non-communication. It gave me a greater insight into her past, and enabled me to let things go that were necessary to release. As a result of therapy, I was able to truly grieve her passing, and have a healthy relationship with her memory today. It has also enabled me to write my story and share it with you. It gave me a barometer on which to reclaim myself. Therapy was a taboo subject, ten to twenty years ago. Our parents' generation viewed it as quaky, off-limits, or just plain weird. "Why not just suck it up?" was their typical response. Many viewed therapy as a sign of weakness.

Because of therapy, I now have lines of communication with my family that did not exist until recently. I always tell them that I love them and that they are important to me. This openness was not something I learned as a child. It was something I had to learn as an adult. When you love someone, you speak it. I firmly believe that seeing a mental health

professional is one of the best gifts you can give yourself.

In 2004, relatively new into my renewed spiritual
quest, I read, *Seat of the Soul*, by Gary Zukav. The
book had been given to me as a gift several years
before. I finally took the time to sit down and read it.
Perhaps somewhere in the back of my mind, I had
hoped to find that I wasn't that far off the path. That
in spite of my years of spiritual sleep, I was all right,
but I found the book challenging and difficult. At
times, it was even uncomfortable and frustrating.
Through that book, I realized just how far off the
mark, I truly was. I came to realize that I had been
living on the body and ego level for years without any
attention to its relationship to my inner self. This
saddened and disappointed me. I was thirty-five, had
grown up in church, held a BA in religion, and had
two years of graduate level work in seminary. I had
always considered myself a godly person, and yet, I
came to realize that I was completely clueless.

The book, challenged me to open my heart,
mind, and spirit in new ways. My reason for getting
frustrated was due in part to where I was and where I
wanted to be. The chasm seemed huge. Luckily, I had
a therapist who thought along the same lines as Gary
Zukav. In a session, I discussed the book and my
disappointment with myself. My therapist gave me
some of the best advice. He told me, "enjoy the view
from where you are now. Look back to see how far
you have come and then look ahead to see where you
are going. You are right where you need to be at this
moment. Be at peace with that." These were timely

words. We've all heard, "It's not the destination; it's the journey."

Quite often, we don't realize we need help until we get help. In whatever you may be dealing with, I encourage you to talk to someone. Acknowledge when you need guidance and ask for it. It is a sign of strength to acknowledge that we don't have all the answers. "No man is an island."

The benefits of therapy and counseling have been well documented by research. They include:

- Learning better ways to handle stress
- Being able to talk through and resolve issues
- Learning better communication skills
- Improved quality of life
- Fewer conflicts
- Improved relationships
- Overcome depression
- Ability to let go of the past
- Improved sense of well-being
- Process of self-discovery
- Learning how to deal more effectively with life's situations
- Being more comfortable with oneself
- Development of insight and increased self-awareness

- Better understanding of one's own behavior and the issues that motivate them
- Increased self-confidence and productivity
- Greater sense of vitality and peace of mind
- Attain a better understanding of yourself and your personal goals and values

It seems appropriate to conclude this chapter with the following quote from, *Seat of the Soul*, by Gary Zukav. It reads,

"As you grow aware of your spiritual self and origin, your immortal ness, and you choose and live according to that first and the physical second, you close the gap that exists between the personality and the soul. You begin to experience authentic power."

X

CHAPTER 19

GRACE IN MY OWN TRUTH

Life has become enjoyable again. My renewed relationship with God has a depth and dimension to it that I never thought possible. Because of this, there has been healing on an emotional and spiritual level. A quote by the French writer, Anais Nin, beautifully illustrates what I mean, "The personal life deeply lived always expands into truths beyond itself."

There came a point, when I chose to take the blinders off. I had come to the conclusion that God was much more than a God who would judge me for my sexuality. Why would He, when it was He that created me this way? Why would He desire that I go through life with shame, hatred, and constant self-loathing because of my sexuality? Why do we feel the need to reduce God to such a limited, antiquated, and puritanical place? To make Him anything less is elitist, arrogant, and just plain stupid.

For so many years, I sought my self-worth through the church, its members, and the denomination; not from God himself. This was huge. Then I came to remember that I was one with Him. I now saw a fuller, more encompassing magnitude of spirituality. The funnel, if you will, had been removed. The blinders had finally come off, and I could never go back. This view was too amazing.

My greatest lesson in life was to learn to find my own path. The one that is right and true for me. I think it no coincidence that I was born a triplet, and then being born gay in addition to that. My own identity, and who I am has been my life's quest. I wanted to be more than just a face in the crowd. There had to be more to life than that. I want to be acknowledged and respected for my own unique gifts and talents. I seek to blaze my own path. To experience all challenges. A great deal of this had to do with finding my value through church work, friends, and family. There had always been a sense of obligation to lose myself in service to others. What better way to do this than through committing myself to ministry? The idea of seeking out one's own path was almost viewed as selfish and humanistic.

Dear Abby once wrote, "Pedestals are cold, drafty places on which to live." There was also this belief that I carried for most of my life that I had to be perfect; that I could be this role model of holiness and sanctity. Why I even bothered to buy into such a ridiculous notion still baffles me. I am not perfect. I never have been, and I never will be. Trying to live up to such a claim depletes enthusiasm, vitality, and leaves me in constant disappointment. It's not real. Carolyn Myss, a highly respected author and teacher, once said, "I am a flawed individual." There is such a sense of relief and a huge weight being lifted when one can genuinely say this and believe it. We are not here to never make mistakes or bad choices, we are here to learn from those experiences and be more compassionate as a result of them. As the Bible states, "Let him that is without sin cast the first stone." John 8:7

Today, being a little older and a little wiser, I have learned to make myself happy. And, instead of trying to make others happy, I desire to help them to do this for themselves. We cannot make others happy no matter how hard we may try. It is something they do for themselves. That choice is completely theirs. This lesson has taken me years to grasp.

In *Essential Guide for Healers*, Carolyn Myss states, "We disappoint others when we upset their plans for our lives." No one wants to let down parents, mentors, family, or friends. So we give in to their demands or expectations, all the while, going against our own heart, true desires, and better judgment.

I have often wanted to ask the parents of gay friends why they did not approve of their son or daughter's "choice to be gay?" As if there was a choice. I would ask if they wanted their child to live a life of deception or be less than self-realized simply to make them happy. In my opinion, it is too high a price to pay and too much of a burden to be put on children by their parents. It totally baffles me that some parents even ask for such a sacrifice. Sadly enough, many do, and marriages are entered into under false pretenses and children are brought into the equation.

It is only an attempt to make others comfortable and to feel accepted by society.

One such instance was played out by a friend of mine by the name of Joseph. I met him at the gym shortly after moving to Atlanta. After a few weeks, and several conversations, it came up about my seminary past, former marriage, and newly embarked life as an openly gay man. Joseph, in his mid-forties, told me his own story. He had been a Southern Baptist minister in Delaware, been married for twenty-five years and had five children. All the while, he knew he was gay. He ultimately came out to his wife and kids. He had resigned his pastoral position, and relocated them to Atlanta to pick up the pieces and move forward.

His honesty and obvious pain from having hurt and having disappointed his family was palpable. But he could also no longer live a lie. As we continued to talk, I realized that this same scenario could have easily been mine some twenty years later had I chosen to fake it. I could not. To me it was too counterproductive and emotionally draining. It would have been unfair to my wife and myself. Joseph assured me that he loved his children, and felt so very fortunate to have had them. And in some small way, deep inside, I almost felt slighted that I would never have that same opportunity to father my own children. It was a tradeoff and we each chose the path that we felt we could honor. I could not estimate how many times I have heard this same story over and over again. I honestly believe that the major reason this happens is from a fear of not wanting to disappoint. It has everything to do with an attempt to live up to what others expect of us—especially our parents and family.

My greatest regret would be to look back at my life at sixty or seventy and realize that I have lived it for someone else and not myself. How many people attend law school for their parents' sake when they actually want to be an artist? How many women marry the wrong man because he's the right religion? How many men feel pressured to sign up for the military because it is their father's path? These are questions to ponder. Sadly, many parents project and impose their own desires onto their offspring. Perhaps you are that parent who is guilty of forcing your wishes on your child or wanting to live your dreams through them. Parents, step out of your comfort zone, past your fears, and encourage your child to seek their inner truth. Why not take the time to ask your son/daughter what it is they want out of their own lives? The fact remains, it is their life. It belongs to them.

Sylvia Browne, in her book, *The Other Side and Back,* writes, "The toughest part is leaving the people in our lives better for having known us, without sacrificing ourselves in the process." This is one of the most difficult, yet valuable balancing acts we could ever learn.

X

CHAPTER 20

MY OWN SPACE

The one concept I so desperately needed to grasp in order to evolve into the person I am today is the realization of my own space. What I mean by this is that I started to discover who I am at the very core of myself. It is much greater than my interests, hobbies, likes, dislikes, career, and sexuality. It is the understanding of who I am at the most fundamental level; my essence as a person. It is not about defining myself through family, friends, or the company I keep. It is coming to know myself on the most intimate level. It is an awareness in the quietness and the stillness. It is an appreciation. It is a certainty I embrace during the days of happiness and joy, but also in the times of grief and immense sorrow.

One way to get to this comfortable place is by spending time alone. Get to know yourself and feel at ease with who you are. Why are so many people afraid to spend time by themselves? Read, contemplate, breath, and meditate. I firmly believe that we cannot be in a healthy relationship with another person until we have a healthy relationship with ourselves. It is in these moments alone, without distractions and noise, that we are most able to go within. What do we see? Is that space filled with work, stress, family, children? What happens when we lose a job, our family life changes, or our kids grow up? The distractions are gone. Now, what fills the void? When I left seminary and all the things that I used to identify myself as a person, what did I have left?

I thoroughly enjoy going to movies by myself. From what movie I select, to where I sit, and who I choose to engage in conversation afterward. I love taking road trips alone. It is time allotted just for me and I feel it is extremely healthy. Some of my most enlightening moments and glimpses of brilliance have come while driving alone. Wayne Dyer once said, "You cannot be lonely if you like the person you're alone with."

What is it that we are so desperately seeking when we lose ourselves in a crowd? When we constantly feel the need to have other people with us at all times? What do we feel that we will miss out on? Are we really letting the noise and constant chatter distract us from looking inside and going deep within? I think the reason that many people go through a midlife crisis is because they fear "being" alone. They have never taken the time to think about what it is that they want out of life and what would bring them true happiness.

It's been said that the most important relationship you will ever have is the relationship you have with yourself. Take the time to get to know who you are. The greatest growth and times of immeasurable bliss occur during these very moments. When you get to know yourself, you then allow others to get to know the real you. And when you are the best version of yourself, you bring out the best in other people. Our idea of love and how we demonstrate it comes from within. We can only love others to the degree to which we love ourselves. Embrace yourself on your best of days and your worst of days. Enjoy your own company.

Try taking the time, starting with one day a month, to do exactly what it is that you want. Do not ask anyone's permission or their accompaniment. Cook dinner for yourself. Try a new gourmet recipe. It's about treating yourself as worthy and deserving. Buy some fresh flowers and arrange them just for you. Treat yourself as you would want others to treat you. Take the yoga or exercise class, which you've been putting off. Buy yourself the new watch that you've been eyeing for weeks. Take the cruise that you have always wanted. Do the things that make you feel good about you. Most times, it's not the love we receive from others that is most important; it's the love that we show ourselves.

Neutrality: One of my more difficult lessons in life, but also one of the most rewarding, was to learn the premise of neutrality. It is only something I have come to fathom in the last year or so. I struggle to do it on a daily basis. It is this ability to remain neutral about whatever is going on in your life. Coming from a place of neutrality enables you to see all experiences, whether good or bad, and how they assist in the growth process. It is by no means an easy task, but when learned, can be one of the most liberating experiences.

Throughout this book, I have shared my most difficult struggles. Many times I got so caught up in the situation that I became the situation. I let it consume and devour me with no hope of a way through or out.

In the Quantum Physics realm, that has become more main stream in the last few years; they refer to it as the non-local observer. What this means is to observe yourself and your situation from your higher self. It is a higher perspective of spirit. In all my years of life, it is the most remarkable and profound tool that I have ever been given.

Boundaries: When we begin to create our own boundaries and work to strengthen them, we automatically become more aware of our encroachment upon other people's boundaries. When we have our own boundaries, we are also more open to giving other people their space. If our boundaries are weak or nonexistent, others will siphon off our joy, energy, peace, and happiness. On a subtle level we will wonder, what is going on? Try it for yourself when you are at the movie theater, a party, grocery store, or family gathering.

What do borders and boundaries do? They keep you intact, and others that don't belong, out. **They protect what is rightfully yours.** Claim your space, and your life. If you don't manage your personal space, someone else will. We have all heard the saying that, "Good fences make good neighbors." At one time or another, we have had the experience of someone getting into our space uninvited. It might have been a coworker, unwanted suitor, an in-law, car salesman, or old church lady who always asks if you are married yet. We have probably done this to others ourselves. It is intrusive and a blatant invasion of space. Call it aura, personal space, whatever. It does exist, and it is viable and real. Some people go so far as to be energy vampires. They deplete your energy and emotional reservoir.

Borders are established to make life easier, more productive. We do it in our cars with traffic lanes and in our office buildings with cubicles. No one is allowed to enter unless you invite them. You have the confidence, right, and intellect to own your own space. To regulate it as you feel and see fit. Instead of getting caught up in other people's dramas and issues, we have the choice to reply, "I hope it all works out."

In my last two years of college, I worked at a large church in SC. The church was an hour away and I was constantly in a rush and in a state of panic. I would stress over the thought of being a few minutes late for fear that someone might reprimand me. I had not one boss at the time, but ten different individuals who felt the need to tell me what they expected. Being on staff (on the inside looking out) was an eye-opener. Some of the most relentless and self-serving people I had ever encountered were church members. The tactics some people used in the name of religion and God were terribly disappointing; they would not have gotten away with this in the business world. And on a bad day, I wanted to call up a few of these choice individuals and let them know just what I thought of their past treatment of me. Sometimes you just have to let things go.

My point, do not look for your answers anywhere but within yourself. There are people who will gladly voice their desires and impose their expectations on you. More importantly, ask what it is that you want and expect of yourself. It has less to do with having others look to you and more to do with looking up to yourself.

For a person to become completely whole and living in their full potential, the connection between mind, body, and spirit needs to be realized. I, like many of my gay friends, enjoy going to the gym. And for many years, my primary focus was my physical body and its appearance. I am all for looking good, feeling energetic, and living healthy, but somewhere along the way, I took my focus off my spiritual being, and totally onto my physical. I became obsessed with making my body look the best that it could possibly be.

At one point I was working out seven days a week. I was living as though this physical body and earthly life was all there was. You want to fit in, look the part, and be accepted. The camaraderie, respect, and unity were what I had longed for. It gave me a sense of community. It's akin to the reason people attend church, join country clubs, attend neighborhood gatherings, and have families. It serves a natural and innate need to belong. Throughout it all, there still existed a deep-seated desire to be known as an individual. Fortunately, this kept me in a somewhat realistic mindset and I didn't go completely over-board.

Amusement: The ability to laugh at myself during the most difficult of times has been paramount in the search for me. I love a great sense of humor and it is one of the qualities that I admire most in my friends. It lightens a mood like nothing else can. It shifts negative energy. Even on your worst days, humor can bring lightness in an instant. The capacity to laugh at yourself is a true asset. This ability to not take yourself so seriously at times is a powerful attribute. I invite you to make laughter a priority in your life.

Simplify: Another very helpful and healthy step I took in getting back in touch with my spirituality and getting to know myself was to simplify my life. I took an inventory of those material possessions, relationships, and habits that were holding me back; those things that no longer serve my highest and greatest good. There were ideas, beliefs, perceptions, and some friends that fell by the wayside. It was a necessity. These things were pulling me down instead of lifting me up. They were attachments and distractions that were stifling me and I had to release them. I was making room for the new me. I wanted to be open to contemporary ideas, supportive people, and opportunities that would foster my newfound belief in spirit and in myself.

Most of us fear change. We want our lives, relationships, and daily activities to remain static.
We find security in the known. But over time, we can
easily become complacent and lazy. We begin to ask,
is this really all that life has to offer? Is this as good as
it gets? Sometimes it takes the death of a family
member or close friend to help us realize just how
short life can be. Because of such a loss, there is
generated a new sense of urgency. There is a renewed
desire to live life to the fullest. To do those things that
you've always dreamed of, but never had the courage
to pursue.

This book is my dream come true. Its main
purpose is to ignite and inspire your belief in yourself.
I hope to get you to take a chance. I hope to encourage you to get back into the daily and active
participation of living your dreams. Think of the
times in your past, where you were most optimistic
and motivated about living life to the fullest. Perhaps
it was high school or college graduation. It was a time
when you felt proud and invincible. You felt as if life
was yours for the taking. You believed that anything
you wanted to accomplish was within reach. You
were in charge of your own destiny. How liberating
and exhilarating to feel that way again.

You can, in fact, have that same enthusiasm for
life right now. It can start this very moment.
Reconnect with your life purpose. Re-ignite the fire
within. Manifest the life that you envision. We are the
sole creators of our own destiny. Nothing else has a

more profound impact on our lives than our own belief and confidence in ourselves. Treasure your abilities and your wisdom to make the choices that are right for you. Remember, you only limit yourself.

If you had one final year of life remaining, what would you change? What goals and aspirations would you finally pursue? What distractions in your life would you let go? What emotional clutter would you throw out? What relationships would you mend? What grudges would you release? This scenario of one final year may sound a bit extreme, but it is powerful. It actually puts things in true perspective. I urge you to start living up to your unlimited potential. Go for it. What is your true passion and are you living it? Are you pursuing your dreams and those things that matter most? Follow your heart and your bliss.

Each morning, when we awake, is the moment we choose. Will it be a run-of-the-mill day? An ordinary day where we just go through the motions? Will it be a day where the same old habits and negative traits of our lower self again take their hold without any say-so from us? Or will it be the day that we say enough is enough and decide that we are tired and bored with an ordinary, minimal existence?

Let today be the day that we take a chance. It is a choice to live a life of our own making; a life that sees promise, value, and awareness in each interaction. A higher calling to use our unique gifts to make life the very best it can be. Allow, encourage, and enable others to do the same. We all have a reason and a mission for being here. Seek that out, seize it, and do not let it go.

)(

CHAPTER 21

LEGACY

I want to pose a question. Be reflective and look deep within. What is your legacy? What kind of impact will you make? What message will you leave with others? Will it be the idea that an ordinary and mundane existence was enough for you? That you played it safe and floated through life? That mediocrity is what you sought and settled for? Will your legacy be one of inspiration, enthusiasm and hope? To have left behind the heritage of being true to yourself, with complete certainty, and knowing you lived up to your highest ideal? Will it be said that you stood up for your own life and followed your heart?

Has your corner of the world been changed for the better because of your presence? What impact will you leave? Will it be the size of your house, the car you drove, and the possessions you owned? These are inconsequential. A happy and fulfilled life is more about helping others along the way. The only legacy we truly leave is the one we leave in the hearts and lives of others. Make yours a memoir characterized as being caring, kindhearted, considerate, tolerant, authentic, sympathetic, and charitable. Give of yourself. Make a difference. Do your part in bringing about an awakened world. The decision is completely ours.

Another crucial step in leaving a lasting impression is admitting past mistakes. To own up to and apologize for mistakes is a sign of strength. To admit that we have done wrong is an enormous step in getting back in touch with our true inner self. It shows accountability. It frees our conscience and lightens the heart. It allows us to release all pretense and guilt and live unhindered.

Optimism: One essential tool for living up to one's full potential is a positive attitude. It allows us to experience the good that life has to offer as well as survive the difficulties and tragedies that often accompany our human existence. When we possess an inner sense of optimism, hopefulness, and encouragement, it is much easier to face any challenge that comes our way.

It is also essential that we feel good about the relationship with ourselves. Again, it is the most important relationship we will ever have. Coming from a positive perspective, attracts and allows new opportunities to unfold in our lives. A positive outlook is unmistakable. It is palpable. You can feel it. Others around you will pick up on this and respond in kind.

We have the ability to choose the emotions we have. Coming from a place of optimism also has to do with ceasing to be a victim of our circumstances, and helps us to rise above them. They can only hold us back if we allow them. Had I succeeded at suicide, I feel it would have been a total cop-out on my part. I am now at a very good place in my life, in my body, and in my spirit. The remarkable thing is that each day gets better and better.

This particular mindset is extremely crucial in leaving a dynamic and motivating legacy for others. It creates positive outcomes in our lives, and in our relationships. It powerfully affects how we interact with others and what we allow into our lives. When we own and put forth a positive attitude, good things and situations automatically began to manifest for us. Be a bright light of hope and inspiration. People are looking for this.

I also encourage you to read books concerning spiritual growth and enlightenment. It is comforting to know that there are other people in the world that seek the same fulfilled life as we do. Books and CDs of this sort help to motivate and energize us on this journey. This type of reading helps to expand our minds and opens us up to greater thought and inspiration. Such authors as Wayne Dyer, Deepak Chopra, Gary Zukav, Alan Seale, Louise Hay, and Brian Weiss are just a few of the writers that have been instrumental in my own search for truth.

It also helps to attend a place of worship with people of like-minded faith. This will hearten and sustain your spiritual awakening. In such a place, you can be encouraged, accepted, bolstered, and renewed.

Chapter 22

Reclaiming Your Inner Child

All too often, we allow life to squelch our dreams. Through the grind of daily living, we let dreams drift away, and eventually forget about them entirely. What a shame that we allow such an injustice and disservice to ourselves. I have had plenty of reasons to do this and justify it to myself, or so it seemed: an incomplete seminary education; a marriage that ended after only three months; a sexuality that society has told me for many years is unacceptable and a perversion of nature. I could also use the excuse that the good always finish last, that I'm a nobody from rural South Carolina, and what do I have to offer? What could I have to say, that would cause others to take notice and listen? There are countless reasons why I could give up and call it quits. I would be cheating myself and selling myself short, though. And if you've chosen to quit, you are missing out on life's greatest gift; the gift of yourself.

A very effective means of dealing with the more bleak periods of life is to reclaim the attributes held as a kid. If you spend any amount of time around children, you will see what I am referring to. They have a joy, excitement, and simplicity about life. They are entirely and completely involved in the moment, and nothing else matters. They are completely void of angst or worry about what tomorrow might bring. We can learn much about life from them. Remember what it was like to be a child. What it was like to experience complete wonder about the simplest of things; to view life through the eyes of a child. It's quite easy to get caught up in the flurry of survival, that we completely miss the joy of living that we once embraced as children. Today, reclaim your sparkle, your amusement, your vitality, your eagerness, and your zest. Let today be the day that you experience from a new perspective. It is that simple: you choose to participate again, rather than just observe. Some of my favorite activities that assist in getting me back to my childlike wonder are:

- Going to the circus
- Attending a G-rated movie
- Watching Saturday morning cartoons
- Having a picnic at a park
- Flying a kite
- Dancing around
- Playing in the sand
- Playing in the rain
- Visiting a local theme park
- Buying a hot dog from a street vendor
- Enjoying an ice cream cone

- Eating cotton candy or a candied apple
- Renting a paddle boat
- Giggling and laughing out loud
- Making rice crispy squares
- Spending an hour at a video arcade
- Reading a Dr. Seuss book
- Playing with a wand and liquid bubbles
- Going roller skating
- Eating my favorite childhood cereal
- Eating Spaghetti Os for lunch
- Buying bubble gum out of a bubblegum machine
- Putting together a jigsaw puzzle
- Playing miniature golf
- Playing a favorite childhood board game
- Odering a child's meal that includes a prize
- Enjoying a coloring book and crayons
- Anything that reminds me of being a kid

These are such simple ideas, but the great thing is that they work. Too often as adults, we lose touch with the innocence of life, and the small wonders that made it so enjoyable being a kid. Reclaim your child-like faith. Get back in touch with that eight-year-old inside and get excited about the simple things. Remember what it was like to be a child and live life from that joy again. A whole new way of existence may unfold for you.

CHAPTER 23

I'M STILL STANDING

My mother was a foreigner and married three times. There were instances in our lives when she was seen as less than deserving because of those characteristics. I was aware of this and very protective of her. I am a white male and in the majority by that very definition. I am also a minority because of being gay. I have felt firsthand, what it is to be discriminated against because of something I cannot and will not deny.

I have always been one who pulled for the underdog. Many times throughout my own life I was considered the dark horse or long shot because of who I was. But each day, I consciously choose not to underestimate myself or my value as a person because of my sexuality, mistakes, or society's pressure to conform and be "normal." I choose not to sell myself short and neither should you. Take the difficulties of life and turn them around for good. The underdog can succeed and do it in a powerful way. We delight when an unlikely winner emerges. Let that be you.

Believe in yourself even when others choose not to. The most remarkable people can come from the most modest and unlikely places. We do not have to look far to see real evidence of this. Such remarkable people as Martin Luther King, Coretta Scott King, Jimmy Carter, and Oprah Winfrey come immediately to mind. These are some of the most humanitarian and influential individuals of our time. They came from such humble beginnings, and yet have made such a tremendous and positive impact on our world. They are truly inspiring.

Be a winner in the search for yourself and the vital role that you serve in the big scheme. Don't allow others to count you out simply because of your skin color, gender, accent, heritage, lack of education, medical condition, or sexuality. Do not let anyone or anything distract you from seeking and pursuing your dreams. When someone insinuates or implies that you'll never be able to succeed, let proving them wrong be one of your greatest motivators.

This is the story of finding my own way. It is an introspective chronicle of self-actualization and a coming to terms with my value as a human being, not in spite of my sexuality, but in light of it. It is my return to self-love and a renewed sense of spirit. My Baptist past, which had served an enormous purpose, had to be released. It no longer fit. It was like a shirt that I had worn for many years and then outgrew. I had discovered other attire that was tailored and more suited for my current evolution as a person. This new garment feels wonderful. The fit is better than I ever thought possible.

If I were sitting next to you, I would encourage you with these very words: individual, special, one of a kind, exceptional, extraordinary, incomparable, matchless, peerless, unequaled, unparalleled, unprecedented, and unrivaled. You are all of these. You are an amazing work of art. Know it, trust it, and exemplify it.

Do not give your power away. I have come to the realization that I have to look at the positive side of things. It is who I am. It is all I know. It has served me well. In the past, I felt a need to curb my enthusiasm for life. I did not want to make others feel out of sorts or uncomfortable. I feared being judged. I did not want to be different. But we are here to learn to make ourselves happy and allow others to do the same. The greatest success we can have in life is our own happiness.

Stop seeking your value as a person through your education, salary, job status, physical appearance, health, car you drive, image, clothing, or material possessions. Who are you beyond this? What lies beneath? Do you like what you see? All of these things are wonderful and necessary and definitely make life more comfortable. But you can't take it with you. The big picture is much greater than these things anyway. Instead of trying to constantly keep up with the Jones', find yourself. For this is where true satisfaction and lasting contentment are found.

Look for inspiration in the simplest of things: in a movie, a song, and other people's stories of triumph. It is in these very moments that spirit can speak the clearest and leave the greatest impression. The universe is always working on our behalf, sending us messages of affirmation, hope, and encouragement. All we have to do is choose to see them.

Each Day:

- Be kind
- Let your light shine
- Practice unconditional Love
- Walk in true humility
- Step outside your comfort zone
- Make the world a better place
- Honor the relationships in your life
- Call a service person (cashier, waitress, bank teller) by their first name; people love to be acknowledged and recognized
- Create the life you want
- Quiet your mind
- Take time to be alone and enjoy the silence
- Enjoy your own company
- Offer your unique gifts to the world
- Practice random acts of kindness
- Be the real deal in your life
- Dream a little higher
- Seek to improve yourself
- Take time to laugh
- Release yourself from the fears of "what if?"

- Open yourself to the miracles of life
- Live a life of distinction
- Take a chance on love again
- Help others along the way
- Choose to see the best in yourself and other people
- Be the best version of yourself
- Forgive and forget
- Revel in your strengths rather than your weaknesses
- Respect yourself
- Pursue your joy
- Know yourself more deeply
- Give away a smile to a total stranger
- Be open to receive
- Make it a pleasure for others to be around you
- Consciously harness the energy of your thoughts and moods
- Instead of being your own worst enemy, be your own best friend

Dave Pelzer, in his book, *Help Yourself*, writes, "Nothing can dominate or conquer the human spirit." You can let the events of your past stifle or propel you to greater personal growth. Take an inventory of your life and the difficulties that you have endured. Find comfort and strength in knowing that you are completely capable of overcoming any situation that you might face. You can do anything that you put your mind to. Be proud of who you are. Love yourself. Believe in whom you are and others will believe in you.

Jeremiah 29:13 reads, "And you shall seek me, and find me, when you shall search for me with all your heart." God's plan for us is much greater than we could ever imagine. Finding your purpose is not always easy. You must embrace life wholeheartedly, explore many different pathways, and allow yourself to grow. Each day, give thanks for the freedom to discover who you are and the self-confidence to embrace it. Do not take your eyes off your dreams. You can make them happen.

Free yourself of regret and self-pity. Begin to heal. Change your view. Make your life a priority. Learn to experience from a higher, more spiritual and loving place. Get back in touch with living from your heart. **Be accountable to yourself. Know who you are.**

)(

CHAPTER 24

HERE'S WHO I AM

I must confess that after some thirty years of being a so-called Christian, it was not until recently that I released the rigid and legalistic mindset that is often associated with the term. A new day has come and my relationship with God is more real now than it has ever been. Instead of being a Christian, I now strive to be Christ-like. Instead of seeing every thing as black or white, I now allow room for beautiful, vibrant color. Instead of looking for the bad in other people, I now choose to see the good. Instead of trying to force others into a box that might make me feel more comfortable, I strive to accept all people as they are. I endeavor to treat them as I want to be treated. Instead of being forced back into that same confining box by society, I now boldly leave it for good. I choose to be me. This capacity has much to do with being comfortable in my own skin and with myself. When we get to this place, we are able to extend the same courtesy to others; to be who they are. Wayne Dyer once said, "When you judge another, you do not define them, you define yourself."

When I was a little boy, I honestly thought that being born black or white was just the luck of the draw. Just as one could be born with brown hair and green eyes, male or female, twin or triplet, one could also be born black or white or anywhere in between. It was something your parents had no control over. Skin color was just another physical trait but not a defining one. Your skin color had little to do with that of your parents'. Both of them might be black and you could be born white. Or you could have two white parents and be born black. There would be no differentiation and no one color was more important than another. Families would be comprised of children of all colors and each loved equally. Again, I thought it was just another random physical characteristic and not some basis on which to discriminate. Do you get my point? Why we make such a huge deal about the pigment in a person's skin is beyond me. It is inconsequential. It's only packaging anyway. In reality, we are all one.

Who I choose to call my companion, partner, confidant, and soul mate is my choice. Who I sleep beside at night and wake up next to in the morning is for me to decide. I seek the same values and traits in my own partner that you cherish in your husband, wife, boyfriend, or girlfriend. Those qualities like honesty, integrity, honor, sincerity, and compassion. These are just as important to me as they are to you. I would ask that you allow others the same opportunity to find love and happiness; the same love that you seek in your own life. Is that so wrong? Show the same kindness, respect, and consideration for their relationship that you demand of your own. As a gay man, why should I deserve or expect any less? Look past the small differences, and instead opt to see the similarities.

My Observations about life thus far:

- You are responsible for your own happiness

- Happiness is a conscious choice

- Stop trading your happiness for someone else's approval

- Everything we need for success and inner joy lies within

- Seek admiration in yourself first, and then it will naturally come from others

- It is important to fill your life with love and laughter

- The way you feel about yourself dictates the type of people that you attract into your life

- When you seek out, develop, and embrace your own unique identity, it will encourage others to do the same

- Be true to whom you are—why would anyone want you to do any less?

- Give others the space they need to find their own inner selves—don't take away their life's lessons

- We are irreplaceable
- Love watches over us
- Carve out your own path in life
- Life is most enjoyed when lived in the moment
- We set the gauge for what we allow to come into our lives
- Cry when you feel sad and when you feel elated
- The power of intention is unmistakable— let it work for you
- You create your own destiny
- Let living from your heart be your greatest achievement yet
- There is hope
- There is peace that passes all understanding
- Instead of being part of the problem, be part of the solution
- God's love sees no differentiation—why can't we?
- Instead of looking for reasons to be offended, look for opportunities to show love
- All things are possible
- Go for it
- One person can make a difference

- Make your life a compelling story
- Whatever you do in life, do it with passion and to the best of your ability
- Simplify your life—instead of seeking value in the material, seek it from within
- Let your life be the pulpit from which you share a message of love, hope, and acceptance for all people

I have written the book that I wished was available when going through my own coming out and discovery process. There were countless times that I questioned my spirituality, worth, and value as a person. Through it all, I found enormous comfort in the following verse, "Being confident of this very thing, that he which hath began a good work in you will perfect it until the day of Christ Jesus." Philippians 1:6

I hope you walk away with a renewed sense of vigor and courage for your own spiritual path.

May you also strive for a greater level of compassion for all people and be more accepting of the diversities that exist. Seek to always come from a place of love. You have the capacity.

If you take anything from my story, let it be the knowledge that you are in fact, unique. Never has there been a person like you with your rare qualities, traits, and gifts. And never again will there be. You are a beautiful creation of God and you have a specific reason for being in this world that no one else can serve. Your highest calling is to find that purpose and embrace it. My hope is that you will look within for appreciation, approval, and validation. Only you can truly fill these needs for yourself. Take time to consider your strongest and most admirable traits. So often, this world has a way of diminishing our self-worth, and what we have to offer. When someone says, "It's been done before," respond with, "Yeah, but not BY ME."

We need to remind ourselves each morning how exceptional we are. When this knowledge comes from within, no one can take it away. You do not have to ask for permission to live your life or apologize for who you are. Celebrate your ability to love, dream, create, empathize, relate, connect, and bond. Cherish your creativity, drive, and passion for life. Think for yourself. Revere your own mind, heart, and spirit. Recognize the phenomenal potential that lies within.

There was a reason I was born as one of a set of triplets to a German immigrant. There was a reason I was born gay, entered seminary, got married, and did not succeed at killing myself. These things have led to the discovery of my *self*.

There is a reason I am still here. There is a reason you are still here. There is a purpose for my writing this book. There is a purpose for your reading it. My hope is that this story has been an encouragement to others who are going through this same journey of self-discovery. It is also meant to be a consolation for those who are experiencing great uncertainty in their lives. It is for those individuals who are trying to figure things out and find their place in it all. I assure you, it is an odyssey worth the taking and I applaud you. I support you in becoming more of your *self*. It is time to seek out your own answers, and your own truth. Let today be the day that you cease to follow someone else's script for your life and began to write your own. You are capable. And always remember, it is good to color outside the lines. In fact, I encourage it. So often, we spend our entire lives just trying to *fit in*, when we were really meant to *stand out*.

ABOUT THE AUTHOR

Mark D. Hyde is a native of Sumter, SC. He graduated from North Greenville College in Tigerville, SC with an Associate of Arts Degree in 1988 and Gardner-Webb College in Boiling Springs, NC with a Bachelor of Arts Degree in Religion in 1990. He attended the New Orleans Baptist Theological Seminary from 1990 until 1992 where he pursued a Master of Divinity Degree in Pastoral Ministries. He was a chaplain and held various church positions throughout his college and seminary years. He has over thirteen years of experience as a recruiter in both the medical and engineering fields.

Mark currently resides in Atlanta, Georgia.

HELPFUL WEBSITES

www.QuantumThink.net

www.TheSecret.TV

www.WhatTheBleep.com

www.AlanSeale.com

www.HayHouse.com

www.DailyOm.com

www.RSIntl.org

www.SLC-Atlanta.org

www.Unity.org

www.UUA.org

www.MCCChurch.org

TO CONTACT MARK

To contact Mark or to schedule a
book club or speaking engagement:

visit:

www.ColoringOutsideLines.com

Or email him at:

MarkCOTL@aol.com